# ATONEMENT:

IN

TYPE, PROPHECY, AND ACCOMPLISHMENT.

By F. W. Grant.

"*A propitiation, through faith, by His blood, to show His righteousness.*" (Rom. iii. 25, *R.V.*)

WIPF & STOCK · Eugene, Oregon

Wipf and Stock Publishers
199 W 8th Ave, Suite 3
Eugene, OR 97401

Atonement
In Type, Prophecy, and Accomplishment
By Grant, F. W.
Softcover ISBN-13: 978-1-7252-7559-1
Publication date 3/30/2020
Previously published by Loizeaux Brothers,

# Contents.

|  |  |  | PAGE. |
|---|---|---|---|
| Chap. | I. | The Need to be Met | 1 |
| " | II. | The Last Adam and the New Creation | 10 |
| " | III. | The Seed of the Woman. (Gen. iii. 15.) | 21 |
| " | IV. | The Ark and the Altar. (Gen. vi. 14–viii. 22.) | 29 |
| " | V. | The Offering of Isaac. (Gen. xxii.) | 36 |
| " | VI. | The Passover and the Sea. (Ex. xii. 14.) | 42 |
| " | VII. | The Tabernacle-Service. (Ex. xxv.–xxx.) | 50 |
| " | VIII. | The Burnt-Offering. (Lev. i.) | 59 |
| " | IX. | The Peace-Offering | 71 |
| " | X. | The Sin-Offering. (Lev. iv.–v. 13.) | 75 |
| " | XI. | The Trespass-Offering | 84 |
| " | XII. | The Two Birds. (Lev. xiv. 1–7; 49–53.) | 90 |
| " | XIII. | The Day of Atonement | 96 |
| " | XIV. | The Red Heifer. (Num. xix.) | 111 |
| " | XV. | Prophetic Testimony. (Isa. vi.; lii. 13–liii.) | 115 |
| " | XVI. | The Testimony of the Psalms | 122 |
| " | XVII. | Atonement in the New Testament. The Gospels | 134 |
| " | XVIII. | Romans and Galatians | 142 |
| " | XIX. | Colossians, Ephesians, 2 Corinthians | 149 |
| " | XX. | Hebrews | 156 |
| " | XXI. | The other Apostolic Writings | 161 |
| " | XXII. | What Christ Suffered in Atonement | 166 |
| " | XXIII. | The Penalty in its Inner Meaning | 177 |
| " | XXIV. | Redemption and Atonement | 187 |
| " | XXV. | Resurrection the Sign of Complete Atonement | 196 |
| " | XXVI. | Union and Identification with Christ | 203 |
| " | XXVII. | God Glorified and Glorifying Himself | 209 |

# Atonement:

IN

## TYPE, PROPHECY, AND ACCOMPLISHMENT.

---

### Chapter I.

*The Need to be Met.*

THE cross of Christ is the central fact in the history of man. To it all former ages pointed on; from it all future ones take shape and character. Eternity, no less than time, is ruled by it: Christ is the "Father of Eternity." (Isa. ix. 6, *Heb.*) The new creation owns Him as last Adam, of whom the failed first man was but the type and contrast. The wisdom, the grace, and the glory of God are displayed, for the ceaseless adoration of infinite hosts of free and gladsome worshipers, in this work and its results.

The doctrine of atonement is thus the centre and heart of divine truth. Unsoundness here will be fatal to the character of all that we hold for truth, and in exact proportion to the measure of its unsoundness. Again, all fundamental error elsewhere will find, of necessity, its reflection and counterpart in some false view of atonement, if consistently carried out. Thank God, this is often not the case, because the heart is often sounder than the creed; but this, while admitted fully, scarcely affects, for a Christian, the seriousness of such a consideration.

In taking up this subject for examination, we must remember the gravity of such a theme; one in which a mere critical spirit will be as much at fault as out of place; where we must be, not judges, but worshipers, yet thoroughly alive to the importance of testing by the Word of God every thing presented. The blessedness of a devout and believing contemplation of the work to which we owe our all will be at least proportionate to the gravity of error as to it; while our preservative from this will be found, not in neglect or slight treatment of so great and important a truth, but in deeper, more attentive and prayerful consideration.

Here, too, we have to avoid, as elsewhere, the opposite dangers of an independent and a weakly dependent spirit. We dare not call any man master, for One is our Master, even Christ. On the other hand, and for that very reason, we dare not despise *His* teaching, even were it from the babe. There is need continually to remind ourselves of this, simple as it surely is. For while the multitudinous voices of christendom rebuke our belief in the authority which they claim, we cannot doubt that the Spirit of truth has been communicating truth in proportion to the simplicity of the faith that trusted Him. We may listen to and gain by teachers just in the measure that we realize the apostle's words, that we have an unction from the Holy One, and need not that any man teach us.

Let us take up, then, the great subject before us, and see reverently what we may be able to learn from Scripture as to it, not refusing to consider along with this, as it may seem profitable, current views, not for controversy on a theme so sacred; testing for the gold and not the dross. The failure of others, where we may have to judge they fail, should surely only serve the purpose of making us cling more humbly, but not less confidently, to the Hand that alone can lead us safely. Just as the works of God need the Sustainer still, so does the word of revelation still need the Revealer.

Before we come to consider the fact and truth of atonement, we have need, first of all, to consider the necessity that exists for it. That it was absolutely necessary, Scripture settles decisively for him that will listen to it. "For as Moses lifted up the serpent in the wilderness, so MUST also the Son of Man be lifted up, that whosoever believeth on Him should not perish, but have everlasting life." Nothing can be plainer, nothing more authoritative, than such an announcement from the lips of Him who came into the world to meet the need that He declares. Whatever is implied in that lifting up of the Son of Man,—the cross, most assuredly,—was necessary for man's salvation: and that the cross was an atonement, or propitiation, for our sins, I need not pause to insist on now.

But while the necessity of the cross is thus put far beyond dispute for all such as I am writing for at this time, it is still needful to inquire, What is the nature of that necessity. It is to our need that God reveals Himself, and as meeting it, while more than meeting it, that He has glorified Himself forever; and to know His grace, we must know the state to which it answers. It is thus that through repentance we come to faith in the gospel. Scripture alone gives the knowledge, in any adequate way, even of man's condition; it is well if we do not resist God's judgment when He has given it.

Man is a fallen being: "all have sinned; and all are "by nature children of wrath." In the order of statement, in that epistle which takes up most fully what we are, as prefatory to the unfolding of that salvation which is its theme, the first is insisted on first, and as if wholly independent of the other. Men excuse their sins by their nature, with how little truth their own consciences are witness; for what they excuse in themselves they condemn in another, and especially if it be done against themselves. God has taken care that within us we should carry a voice which sophistry can never completely silence, and which asserts our responsibility, spite of our natures, for every sin of our hearts or lives. In that day to which conscience ever points, "the day when God shall judge the secrets of men by Jesus Christ," He "will render to every man according to [not his *nature*, but] his *deeds*." And for which of his *deeds* could he excuse himself with truth by the plea that he could not help it? Surely not for one. The free-will of which man boasts comes in here to testify fearfully against him. His nature, whatever its corruption, is not, *in the sense in which he pleads*, prohibitory of good or obligatory to evil. Conscience, anticipating the righteous judgment of God, refuses to admit the validity of such a plea. It is the intuitive conviction of every soul that sins, that for that sin it is justly liable to judgment.

On this ground it is that the law brings in—

every man for his own sins,—"all the world guilty before God." In all that part of Romans, from the first to the middle of the fifth chapter, in which this as to man is taken up, the apostle will raise no question as to his nature,—speaks as yet no word of Adam or the fall. Before he can bring it forward at all, it must be absolutely settled that as all have sinned, so "all have come short of the glory of God." That which for Israel the impassable vail of the holiest declared, is what is affirmed by the gospel as to all, without exception. It is upon this common basis of judgment lying upon all, that justification for the ungodly is proclaimed to all.

The question of nature comes in in the second part of the epistle, in connection with the power for a new life. It is after man's guilt, proved to be universal, is met, for all that believe, by the precious blood of Christ, and "being justified by faith, we have peace with God," our standing in grace, "and rejoice in hope of the glory of God," that the apostle goes on to compare and contrast the first Adam and his work with Him of whom he is the type: "Wherefore as by one man sin entered into the world, and death by sin, and so death passed upon all men, for that all have sinned; . . . therefore as by the offense of one [or by one offense] toward all men to condemnation, so by one righteousness toward all men for justification of life. For as indeed by the disobedience of the one man the many have been constituted sinners, so also by the obedience of the One the many will be constituted righteous." (I quote this from a version more literal than our common one, which is very faulty here.) Afterward, this corruption of constitution is fully dealt with, and the remedy for it shown; but of this it is not yet the place to speak.

It is evident, however, that this increases the gravity of man's condition immensely. The apostle, following the Lord's own words to Nicodemus, calls this fallen nature of man flesh, stamping it thus as the degradation of the spiritual being which God had created, hopeless naturally, as the Lord's words imply: "That which is born of the flesh is flesh." The apostle states it thus: "The mind of the flesh is enmity toward God, for it is not subject to the law of God, neither indeed can be; so then they that are in the flesh cannot please God."

With the many questions which spring out of this we are not now concerned; but such are the solemn declarations of Scripture, with which all the facts of observation and experience coincide. For man thus guilty and alienated from God, atonement is necessary ere there can be mercy. "Deliver him from going down into the pit" must have this as its justification: "I have found a ransom."

The penalty upon sin is the necessary expression of His essential holiness. He can neither go on with sin nor ignore it; and this is a question not alone of His government, but of His nature also. To be a holy *governor*, He must be a holy God. Government would be simply impossible for God that did not represent aright His personal character. If, then, in His government He cannot let sin escape, it is because the holiness of His nature forbids such an escape. This we shall find to be of very great importance when we come to the consideration of what the atonement is; but it is important to realize from the outset. Law, whatever its place, can never be the whole matter; while yet its enactments must be in harmony with the deeper truth upon which it rests.

"To men it is appointed once to die, but after this the judgment." This is the inspired statement as to what he naturally lies under. Both these things have to be considered in their character and meaning, for as to both of them many a mistake has been made.

Death entered into the world by the sin of Adam. It is not necessary to take this as applying to the lower creatures. No express word of Scripture affirms this, and the whole web and woof of nature seems to contradict the thought. Life, without a miracle to prevent it, must be destroyed continually, apart from all question of carnivorous beasts or birds, by the mere tramp of our feet over the earth, in the air we breathe, the water we drink, the plants or fruits we consume. The herbivorous animals thus destroy life scarcely less than the carnivorous. Scripture, too, speaks of the "natural brute beasts" as "made to be taken and destroyed," and of "man being in honor and understanding not becoming *like* the beasts that perish." But unto the world—the human world,—by one man sin entered, and death by sin; "and so death passed upon *all men* [he speaks only of man], for that all have sinned." It is the stamp of God's holy government upon sin; the outward mark of inward ruin.

This death which came in through sin we must distinguish from the judgment after death, as the apostle distinguishes them in the text already quoted. This has not always been done, and yet not to do it is to make difficult what is simple, and to obscure not a little the perfection of the divine ways. The sentence upon Adam was not a final sentence, but one in which the mercy is evident amid all the severity of righteous judgment. Without the ministration of death, sad as has been the history of the world, it would have been much sadder; but upon this I do not now need to pause. The sentence on Adam is sufficiently clear from what is actually passed upon him after the transgression, and whose meaning no one can doubt:—"Until thou return unto the ground; for out of it wast thou taken; for dust thou art, and unto dust shalt thou return." Of the second death this may be, and is, a type, and a warning: but no more.

Again, to confound the penalty upon sin with sin itself would seem almost impossible did we not know that it had been really done. It is true that man's sinful state is spoken of as death—a "death in trespasses and sins." But unless God could inflict sin as such, which is impossible, this would turn the penalty into a prophecy merely. The testimony of conscience should be enough in such a case; but the words of the sentence when actually given, as I have just now quoted them, should preclude the possibility of doubt.

Yet here too it is a type—the outward manifestation of the state to which it answers; for as the body without the spirit corrupts into sensible abomination, so with man away from God.

Death is judgment; to the natural man, how solemn an one! smiting him through the very centre of his sensitive being, and sending him forth from every thing he knows and values into a gloom surcharged with the foulness of corruption, and with the terrors of God, to which he goes forth naked and alone.

Death is judgment, but not "*the* judgment." For this, the "resurrection of judgment" must have come in,—judgment claiming for this the body as well as the spirit—the whole man, in short. And here, that separation from God, chosen by the soul itself, becomes manifest in its true horror, and its definitive portion forever. This is the "outer darkness," when God the light of life is withdrawn forever.

But not in every sense withdrawn. For the second death is not only darkness, though it is darkness. The second death is none the less the "lake of fire:" a figure indeed, but none the less fearful because a figure: "our God is a consuming fire." Worse than withdrawn, the light has become fire. For God cannot forget, cannot simply ignore: where sin is, there must be the testimony of His undying anger against it. Here, "according to the deeds done in the body," there is the searching, discriminating apportionment of absolute righteousness.

Death then, and after death the judgment: this is man's natural portion; these are the two things from which he needs to be delivered. For judgment he cannot abide; if he dream of the possibility of it, it is but a dream: "Enter not into judgment with Thy servant, O Lord; for in Thy sight shall *no man living* be justified." This is what Scripture with one voice affirms. If it were but believed, how many wrong thoughts would it not set right! how many theological systems would it not utterly sweep away!

This, then, is the portion of man as man: this is the burden that atonement has to lift from off him.

## Chapter II.

*The Last Adam and the New Creation.*

WE are going to look at the truth of atonement in the way in which Scripture develops and puts it before us; beginning with the Old Testament and proceeding, in the regular order of its books as we have them, onward to the New; except that we shall necessarily take the light of the New Testament to enable us to read the Old-Testament lessons aright, remembering that the "vail is done away in Christ." I choose this method, rather than what might seem the simpler one, of stating the doctrine after the manner of the creed or theological text-book, for many reasons.

God's method of teaching plainly has not been by the creed. He could surely have given one, not only better than any human could claim to be, but absolutely perfect, avoiding all the errors and all the incompleteness of the best of creeds, and giving what would be indeed a royal road to knowledge in divine things. It has pleased Him otherwise; and in this there must be wisdom worthy of Him, and care too for the real need of His people. God's way has been to speak to us in a far different manner. He has given us truth in fragments, which at first sight seem even to have little orderly connection,—which gleam out upon us from history, psalm, and prophecy, as well as in more detached statement sometimes in an apostolical epistle. Even here we have seldom what the systematic theologian would call a treatise;

certainly nothing at all resembling the articles of a confession of faith or of a creed.

Understand me, I am not denying that such things have their place. Unfortunately they are valuable precisely when stripped of that in which to most lies all their value. As authoritative expositions of doctrine, they substitute human authority for divine; the confession, with all its admitted liability to error, in place of the unfailing, infallible Word, by which the Holy Spirit, the sure and only Guardian of the Church in the absence of Christ its Head, works in the hearts and consciences of men. Stripped of the false claim, and left as the witness of what individual faith has found in the inspired Word, they may be used of God as the voice of the living witness. However, to that Word, with all its perplexities of interpretation, as men speak, we must come for that which can alone give certainty to the soul; these very perplexities used of God to give needful exercise, to deepen the sense of dependence upon Him, and discipline us by the exercise.

The truth given in this way, moreover, only to be learnt fragment by fragment, by constant research into and occupation with the precious book in which the treasure lies, enforces its lessons by that needful frequent "putting in remembrance" of which an apostle speaks. We realize its many sides and internal relationships; we discern how little all our systems are, compared with the truth itself; that the completeness we desired was only narrowness. Finally, that God's method of teaching is divine, as the truth taught is; His way to lead us out, at least into more apprehension of the infinity of that which, cramped into the human measure, necessarily becomes dwarfed and distorted by it.

In the historical part of the Old Testament, the lessons given to us are mainly those pictured lessons which we call types. But before we come to the types of atonement proper, there is one we must consider, which, although not that, is in the deepest and most intimate relation to it, and the right or wrong conception of which will influence correspondingly our view of atonement itself. The apostle tells us, with regard to the first man, that Adam was "a figure of Him that was to come" (Rom. v. 14.); and in 1 Cor. xv. 45, he speaks of Christ as the "last Adam." He is again spoken of by the same apostle as the "First-born of every creature," or, "of all creation" (Col. i. 15.); and speaks of Himself, in the address to Laodicea, as the "beginning of the creation of God." (**Rev. iii.14**) So again, "If any one be in Christ, he is a new creature [or, "it is new creation"]: old things are passed away; behold, all things are become new" (2 Cor. v. 17.); and this is insisted on as the governing principle of a Christian life; "for in Christ Jesus neither circumcision availeth any thing, nor uncircumcision, but a new creation; and as many as walk according to this rule, peace be on them, and mercy." (Gal. vi. 15, 16.)

The fallen first man and the old creation are thus, according to God's thought, replaced by the last Adam and a new creation. There is no restoration of the old; it is set aside, or becomes the material out of which the new creation is to be built up; and this last is God's creation—what was in His mind from the beginning. So, when the Psalmist asks, "What is man, that Thou art mindful of him? or the son of man, that Thou visitest him?" the answer is, "Thou madest him a little lower than the angels, Thou hast crowned him with glory and honor." This the apostle interprets for us in the epistle to the Hebrews,—" But we see Jesus, who was made a little lower than the angels for the suffering of death, crowned with glory and honor."

This last Adam, true man as He surely is, is emphatically the "Second Man." "The first man Adam was made a living soul; the last Adam was made a quickening spirit." "The first man is of the earth, earthy; the Second Man is of heaven [so all the editors read it now]. As is the earthy, such are they also that are earthy; and as is the heavenly, such are they also that are heavenly. And as we have borne the image of the earthly, we shall also bear the image of the heavenly." Here, as elsewhere, the type is the shadow only, and therefore in many things the contrast, of the antitype; and so precisely as to what is connected with each.

Here is the great and fundamental mistake with the general mass of theological systems. They make the first man God's real thought instead of the Second, and bring Christ in to restore the first creation; to gain what Adam should have gained or kept. Thus many now think of no more than earthly blessing for the saint, while those who are not able to resign their heavenly inheritance would make this Adam's natural birthright also. The so-called evangelical creeds of christendom put Adam under the moral law to win heaven for himself and his posterity, and write "This do, and thou shalt live" over the gate of entrance. The Lord's suffering in death, they say, puts away our sins; His obedience to the law is our title to heaven. But in this way, not only is the full blessedness of the Christian's place unknown, but Christ's work is necessarily however unintentionally degraded.

To Adam in Eden God spoke nothing of heaven, nor ever connected going to it with the keeping of the law. "This do, and thou shalt *live*," He did say; never, "This do, and thou shalt go to heaven." God never proposed to the creature He had made to win by His obedience a higher place than He had put him in at first. To have proposed it would have been to have made man from the start what sin has so long made him—a worker for himself rather than for God. He who has said, "When ye have done all, say, We are unprofitable servants," could never have taught him any thing so perilously like a doctrine of human merit.

Under law Adam was, as is evident; but not under the moral law, which an innocent being could not even have understood. The commandment to him was simply not to eat of the tree of the knowledge of good and evil; the terms, not "This do, and thou shalt live," but "Do this, and thou shalt die." He had not to seek a better place, but enjoy the place he had. Men may reason and speculate, but they cannot find one word of Scripture to justify the thought that unfallen Adam was what sin has made man now—a stranger, or what grace has made the saint—a pilgrim. He was made to abide, and his punishment not to abide, where God had put him.

It is to man fallen, not innocent, that God speaks of heaven; and by grace, not law at all. It is the fruit of another's work, who, not owing obedience for Himself, as a creature must, could give thus to what He undertook, a real and infinite merit. Christ's work alone has opened heaven to man; the value of the work being according to the value of Him whose work it is. Apart from any question of the fall, the first and the last Adam are in this way contrasts: "the first man Adam was made a living soul; the last Adam was made a quickening spirit;" "the first man is of the earth, earthy; the Second Man is the Lord from heaven;" or rather, as the editors read it now, "the Second Man is of heaven."

Here the first man, as a type, images however the Second, where God breathes into his nostrils the breath of life. This is an essential difference between man and the beast below him: he has by the inspiration of God what the beast has not; and thus Elihu has the justification of his claim. That his "lips shall utter knowledge clearly" refers back to the original creation: "The Spirit of God hath made me, and the breath of the Almighty hath given me life." In the doctrine of Scripture elsewhere we find distinctly what the breath of the Almighty has given to man which distinguishes him from the beast. It is the "spirit of man which is in him," and by which alone he knows the things of a man. (1 Cor. 2. 11.) He has a spirit, as "God is spirit," and thus by creation, as Paul quotes from the Greek poet to show the general sense of man, declares, "We are God's offspring."\*

And yet "the first man Adam was made a living soul," as this history in Genesis itself declares—"Man became a living soul." In this he was what

---

\* See "Facts and Theories as to a Future State," or "Creation in Genesis and in Geology," for a full exposition of this.

the beasts were. In this, Scripture anticipates all that is real in what the science of the day vaunts as its own discovery. Man is as the beast is, a being bound within the limits of sense-perception, through which all the stores of the knowledge upon which he so prides himself have to be painfully acquired. The spirit of man is in this way, by the necessity of his nature (I speak not of the fall), subjected to the soul. And the apostle connects this, in the passage before us, with the possession of a "natural body," as he does the "spiritual body" of the resurrection with the "image of the heavenly" last Adam. This "natural body" is rather, literally, a soul-body (the English language has no adjective for "soul"),— that is, a body fitted for the soul, as the spiritual body will be for the spirit. Hence it is that with the body the mind grows, and with it languishes and apparently decays; and hence in Scripture the title for one absent from the body is higher than for one in it. *In* the body, he is a "living soul;" *absent* from the body, he is a ghost, or spirit.

From hence arises an important consideration. For while ever the Second Man, and as such "of heaven," it is plain that the Lord was pleased to be subject through His life here, as man, to the conditions of man. Ever "apart from sin," save as in grace bearing it upon the cross, the limitations springing from disease and decay He could not know, of course; but of His childhood we read expressly that He "*grew* in wisdom and in stature,"—mind unfolding with the body as with men in general. How differently inspired Scripture speaks from what a mere human biographer would have written of the "Word made flesh"!

But what such words decisively prove, in opposition to men's thoughts about it, is that while Second Man from the beginning of His human life, as I have said, He ever was, He did not take the place of last Adam until His sacrificial work was finished and in His spiritual body He rose from the dead. "Except a corn of wheat fall into the ground and die, it abideth alone," such are His own words; "but if it die, it bringeth forth much fruit."

This explains the Lord's significant action when after the resurrection He appears to His disciples and, breathing on them, says, "Receive ye the Holy Ghost." For the first Adam had as a living soul been breathed into when quickened of God; the last Adam as a quickening spirit breathes into others. Not, of course, that it was quickening here: they had surely been already quickened; but now He puts them formally into the place of participants in a life now come through death, and to which justification attached as fruit of the death through which it had come. They are to be in a definite place of acceptance and peace with God, according to His words before He breathes on them—"Peace be unto you," twice spoken. "Justification of life" is thus assured to them, the doctrine of which the apostle develops in the fifth of Romans.

The same chapter distinctly brings forward the first Adam as the "figure of Him that was to come." The contrast between the two does not affect the comparison: it is a comparison of contrasts. In the first Adam's case, "through the offense of one the many have died," and "by one that sinned" "the judgment was by one to condemnation;" and "by the disobedience of the one the many have been constituted sinners." The point here is the bearing of the act of the one, the father of the race, upon the state of the many, his children: corruption of nature, death, the present judgment, tending to final condemnation, have come to them in this way. So in the case of the Second Adam has His obedience resulted in blessing to those connected with Him. Only, "not as the offense is the free gift." God is not satisfied with a mere obliterating the effect of the first man's sin, He will go far beyond that in His grace: "If through the offense of one the many have died, much more has the grace of God, and the gift by grace, which is by one Man, Jesus Christ, abounded unto the many." If many offenses have been added by Adam's posterity to the primal sin, "the free gift is of *many* offenses unto justification;" "if by the offense of one death reigned by one, much more shall they which receive abundance of grace and of the gift of righteousness reign in life by One, Jesus Christ."

It is this "much more." of divine grace, which has been so forgotten, and which we must ever bear in mind. *The value of the person of the Second Adam gives proportionate value to His work. The work itself, moreover, is such as none but He could possibly have accomplished. And the value of person and work together gives those in whose behalf it is accomplished a place of acceptance with God of which He Himself, gone into His presence, is the only measure. It is not now the time to speak at large of this, but it is essential to keep it in mind. Christ and the new creation must get their due place for our souls, or all will be confusion.

The two verses which follow in the fifth of Romans we must carefully distinguish in their scope. The eighteenth verse contemplates "*all* men," the nineteenth, the "many" who are connected with the one or the other of these two heads. The first gives us the *tendency* of Christ's work; the second, the actual result. It is as impossible to make the "all men" mean just those in effect saved, as it is to extend the "many" with whom Christ is connected into the whole human race. The *tendency* of the "one offense" was "toward all men to condemnation" (I do not quote the common version, which has here supplied words which the original has nothing of); the tendency or aspect of the "one righteousness," "toward all men to justification of life." On the other hand, in actual result, "as by the disobedience of the one man the many were constituted sinners, so by the obedience of the One the many shall be constituted righteous."

The result contemplates all those, obviously, of whatever age or dispensation, who obtain salvation through our Lord Jesus Christ; and it should be as evident that the connection with Christ that is spoken of is with Him as the last Adam, that is, *vital* connection. The many being constituted righteous gives, I have no doubt, the fullness both of imputed and imparted righteousness. For as the life communicated by the last Adam is necessarily such as He Himself is, so also it carries with it the efficacy of the work accomplished—of the death through which the corn of wheat could alone bring forth fruit. "The gift of God is eternal life *in* Jesus Christ our Lord" (ch. vi. 23, *Greek*): justification is therefore "justification of *life*." These go together. How completely this connection harmonizes with the apostle's argument in the next three chapters will be plain to those who are happily familiar with the doctrine there,—a doctrine which comes in as the answer to the practical question with which they begin: "Shall we continue in sin that grace may abound?" Upon this, however, I cannot enter here.

We are only upon the threshold of the subject which is before us yet, and all that we have done is just to indicate certain connections of atonement, which will find their development as we take up, as we have now to take up, in its gradual unfolding from the beginning, the doctrine of atonement itself.

## Chapter III.

*The Seed of the Woman. (Gen. iii. 15.)*

SIN had no sooner come into the world than God announced atonement for it. If God took up man, become now a sinner, in the way of blessing, He must needs, in care for His own glory, as well as mercy even to man himself, declare the terms upon which alone He could bless. And although He did not and could not yet speak with the plainness or fullness of gospel-speech, yet He *did* speak in such a way as that, (in spite of six thousand years of wanderings further from the light,) the broken syllables echo yet in the traditions of Adam's descendants, in witness to divine goodness, alas! against themselves.

It is in the judgment denounced upon the serpent that we find the promise of the woman's Seed; a promise indeed, as men have ever and rightly held it, though couched in such a form. To Adam as the head of fallen humanity it could not be directly given, for reasons which we have already seen; for in fact the first Adam and the old creation were not to be restored, but replaced by another. The woman also, with the man, was to share only in the fruits of Another's victory, whom grace alone has brought down to the lowly place of the woman's Seed. The announcement is therefore designedly given in the shape of judgment upon the serpent—judgment which is to be the victory of good over evil, the issue of a conflict now in full reality begun. In righteous retribution, through the woman's Seed the destroyer of man should be destroyed; but this is connected with enmity divinely "put" between the tempter and the tempted, in all which God's intervention in goodness for the recovery of the fallen is plainly to be seen. The victory of the woman's Seed is a victory of divine goodness in behalf of man.

This victory is not gained without suffering. The heel that bruises the serpent's head will be itself bruised. The Conqueror must be the Sufferer.

Moreover, the Conqueror is the woman's Seed. We are apt to miss the force of this, just by our familiarity with it. Not yet had the mystery of human birth been accomplished upon earth. The lowliness of origin, the helpless weakness and ignorance of infancy, so long protracted beyond that of kindred bestial life around,—this, by which God would stain the pride of man, was that through which Adam and his wife had never passed. The Seed of the woman implied all this. With what astonishment we may well conceive Satan to have contemplated the childhood of the first-born of the human race; and to have thought of the word, whose certainty he could not doubt (for Satan, the father of lies, is no unbeliever), that the heel of One so born and nurtured was to be one day upon his own proud angelic head!

Not strength was to conquer here then, but weakness—known and realized weakness. Of that the promise spoke. And God, who needed not the help of creature-strength, had chosen to link Himself with weakness and with suffering to accomplish His purposes of righteousness and goodness. How and in what way to link Himself remained for future disclosures to make known.

But that bruised heel, bruised in the act of victory on behalf of others, is not left without further revelation of its nature on the spot. For when Adam's faith, bowing to the divine word, names the woman—her through whom death had entered, —*Havvah* (Eve) or "life;" then we read, "Unto Adam also, and to his wife, did the Lord God make coats of skins, and clothed them." Thus the shame and the fact of their nakedness were together put away. It would now have been unbelief for Adam to say, as with his fig-leaf apron he had still to say, that he was naked. God's own hand had clothed him. No need for him to hide himself from His presence as before. The clothing His hand had given was not unfit to appear in before Him.

But what gave it that fitness? Clearly something apart from suitability in the way of protection of a being naturally defenseless, and now exposed to the vicissitudes of a world disarranged by sin. The nakedness which Adam realized in the presence of God was moral rather than physical, the consciousness of the working of lusts at war in the members. The covering too, then, for God must have some moral significance,—must speak at least of that which would cover, not merely from a human, but from a divine standpoint; therefore put away sin really, for how else could it be "covered" from His sight?

Now, in Scripture, "covering" is *atonement*— *i.e.*, expiation, putting away of sin. To atone is *caphar*, to "cover;" only in an intensive form, which is of striking significance and beauty. Atonement is covering of the completest kind.

We have not the word yet in this first page of the history of the fallen creature, but we have surely what connects with it in a very intelligible way. For death had now come in through sin, and as judgment upon it. Death would remove the sinner from the place of blessing he had defiled, and thus far maintain and vindicate the holiness of God; but in judgment merely, not in blessing. Atone for his sin in any wise such death could not. Yet here is declared the fact that the death of *another*, innocent of that which brought it in, could furnish covering for the sinner according to God's mind. Only the typal shadow yet was this: it was four thousand years too early for the true atonement to be made. Yet shadow it was: would not faith connect it, however dimly, with the bruised heel of the woman's Seed?

In this clothing God's hand wrought, and not man's. God wrought and God applied. Man's first lesson, which it were well if after forty centuries he had really learnt, was, that he could do nothing but submit to the grace which had undertaken for him. The fig-leaf apron had summed up and exhausted his resources, and demonstrated only his helplessness. He had now to find that helplessness made only the occasion of learning the tender mercy of God. God wrought and God applied to these first sinners the covering for their nakedness. And so it has been ever since, and so will be, to the last sinner saved by grace.

But the gospel at the gate of Eden is not finished yet. We must take in, plainly, what the next chapter gives, before we can realize how much already in Adam's days God had, though necessarily as it were in parables, declared.

Abel's offering is that by which, as the apostle says, he, being dead, yet speaketh. "By faith Abel offered unto God a more excellent sacrifice than Cain; by which he obtained witness that he was righteous, God testifying of his gifts; and by it he being dead yet speaketh." In him we are given to see, just at the threshold of the world's history, the pronounced acceptance of a faith which brought, not its own performances, as Cain the labor of his own hands which sin had necessitated and stained, but the substitute of a stainless offering. The character of it shows clearly that sacrifice was an institution of God: "*by faith* Abel offered;" not therefore in will-worship. Nor could human wit have imagined as acceptable to God what, except for its inner meaning, could have had no possible suitability nor acceptance at His hands. The coats of skin, confessedly of His own design, give here indubitable evidence that the whole thought and counsel was of Him. Here again death covers the sinner; but now in proportion to the clearness with which the sacrificial character of the covering comes out, so do we find God's voice plainly giving its testimony to the righteousness of the offerer: "God testifying of his gifts." As with one of His ministers, in a day yet far distant,—but only with regard to bodily healing—the *shadow* of Christ, as here in sacrifice, is of power to heal the soul.

Thus in the order of these two cases the manner and nature of appropriation are plainly seen. First, *God* appropriates the value of Christ's work to the soul; for faith must have God's act or deed to justify it as faith; and then it sets to its seal that God is true. It is not faith's appropriation that makes it true, as some would deem. It is the receptive nature that holds fast merely what God has put already in its possession. To those who take shelter still under the atoning death of the great Victim, God attests its value on their behalf. It is for them to believe their blessedness on the word of One who cannot lie, nor repent.

Let us notice here, as ever henceforth, the victim is of the flock or herd, or what at least is not the object of pursuit or capture; which plainly would not harmonize with the fact of man's lost condition, or with the voluntary offering of Him who freely came to do the will of God. The blood of no wild creature could flow in atonement for the soul of man. The precise commandment as to this comes indeed much later, but to it from the first both Abel's and every other accepted sacrifice conform. Of blood no mention is made either here; of the fat there is: "And Abel, he also brought of the firstlings of his flock, and of the fat thereof;"—the fat being that in which the good condition of the animal made itself apparent. Fat is always in Scripture the symbol of a prosperous condition, although, it may be, of such temporal prosperity as might result in an opposite state of soul. "Jeshurun waxed fat and kicked," says the lawgiver in his last prophetic "song;" "thou art waxen fat, thou art grown thick, thou art covered with fatness: then he forsook God that made him, and lightly esteemed the Rock of his salvation." Connected with this is the Psalmist's description of the wicked: "They are inclosed in their own fat; with their mouth they speak proudly." Then by an easy gradation of thought: "Their heart is as fat as grease." Where offered to God, fat is the symbol of that *spiritual* well-being which expresses itself, not in the energy of self-will, but of devotedness. Even in the sin-offering afterward, where burnt upon the ground, the fat is always therefore reserved for the altar; but of this elsewhere.

The "firstling of the flock" again represents Him who is the "first-born among many brethren" by Him sanctified. "For both He that sanctifieth and they who are sanctified are all of one; for which cause He is not ashamed to call them brethren." The consecration of the first-born sanctifies the whole.

What mind of man could have anticipated thus the thought and purpose of God as does Abel's offering? In it the lesson of the coats of skin is developed into a doctrine of atonement henceforth to be the theme of prophecy and promise for four thousand years, till He should come in whom it should find its fulfillment, and all vail be removed. Until then, prophets themselves knew but little of what they prophesied. "The Spirit of Christ which was in them" spake deeper things than they could even follow, as the apostle testifies; though we must not imagine all was dark.

That sacrifice, on the other hand, was of God's appointment, not of human device, His words to Cain are full proof.—"If thou doest well, shalt thou not be accepted? and if thou doest not well, a sin-offering coucheth at the door." So, I am persuaded, this ought to be read. "Sin" and "sin-offering" are the same word whether in Greek or Hebrew; but what would be the force of "if thou doest not well, sin coucheth at the door"? That the last expression refers to an animal seems plain: some interpreters take it figuratively, as if sin as a wild beast were in the act to spring. Too late, surely, when one has already sinned! Rather would it not be the provision of mercy for one in need of it—an offering not far to seek, but at the very door! and in what follows, the assurance of his retaining still the first-born's place with regard to Abel—"Unto thee shall be his desire, and thou shalt rule over him"?

God thus, then, declares His appointment of sacrifice. And in this way the mystery of the suffering of the woman's Seed finds its explanation in the necessity of atonement. The bruised heel of the Victor in man's behalf enlarges and deepens into the death of a victim, slain for atonement. It is not really the serpent's victory even thus far, though it may seem so: the serpent may bruise the heel, but only as the unwitting instrument of divine goodness in accomplishing man's deliverance. The bruised heel is his own head bruised: the suffering is the victory of the Sufferer.

But who is this, to whom death—and such a death!—is *but* the heel, the lowest part, bruised? What a thought of the majesty of His person is here! Already there is a gleam of the glory of Him whom after-prophecy, supplementing this, shall speak of as the virgin's Son, Immanuel. But the question is only raised as yet, to which Isaiah gives this answer. *We* can see it is the fitting and necessary one.

## Chapter IV.

*The Ark and the Altar.* (*Gen.* vi. 14–viii. 22.)

WE are no more than fairly entered upon our subject as yet; and of all that we have learned hitherto the examination of other scriptures will confirm, extend, and render more precise our knowledge. We have seen the need of man, which atonement has to meet, to be fourfold: first, his actual sins; secondly, corruption of nature; thirdly, the penalty of death, proclaimed by God in Eden, and in which clearly all men share as well as the first sinner; fourthly, the judgment after death. As to this last, so far as we have reached in Genesis, it is rather a dread undefined shadow than a thing plainly taught, an inference rather than an announcement. Correspondingly we find in atonement, so far as we have hitherto gone, the emphasis laid upon *death* as borne by a substitute, —a truly vicarious death, by which sin is "covered" or expiated before God, and the shame of man's nakedness put away.

But yet the one who obtains witness that he is righteous, God testifying of his gifts, and though dying in his substitute, dies *himself*, as all mankind but two have ever done. Why this? Surely because that while atonement is in behalf of sinners of Adam's seed, its purpose is not to restore the first man or the old creation, but to bring those saved into the new. While, of course, as to power over the soul, death *is* "abolished:" "Whosoever liveth and believeth in Me shall never die."

That to which we now come will bring, and is designed to bring, this change from the old to the new creation vividly before us. The ark which Noah prepared to the saving of his house is a figure of Christ, as we surely know, and of Christ as One with whom we pass through the judgment of the world into that new scene where all abides in the value of the accepted sacrifice. "If any man be in Christ, [it is] new creation: old things are passed away; behold, all things are become new."

For faith anticipates that judgment yet to come, meets it in the cross, and passes through it, leaving it behind. The death of our Substitute is for us what death ever is—our passage out of the world. Sheltered and safe ourselves, we pass through it; our Ark alone breasting the flood, and lifted above it by its own inherent buoyancy; for the Holy One could go through death, but not be holden of it. By the might of His own perfection He rose into the sphere to which He belonged, carrying with Him the hopes and promise of the new creation.

The gopher-wood, the material of the ark, I can say little of, but it speaks of death (the tree cut down), as that by which alone death could be met for us. The "pitch" is *copher*, near akin, as it would seem, to *gopher*, not bitumen (or at least there is no proof of this), but, as would seem most probable, a resin from the gopher-wood itself; identical, too, with the word "atonement" in one of its forms.* Here, it seems to me, is the first hint we find in Scripture of something beyond death which is implied in and needed for atonement. Not the gopher-wood alone would have kept out

---

*Translated "ransom," Ex. xxx. 12; 1 Sam. xii. 3, *marg.*; Job xxxiii. 24; xxxvi. 18; Ps. xlix. 7; Prov. vi. 23; etc.; "satisfaction," Num. xxxv. 31, 32.

the waters of judgment. Not death alone lay upon men, and for true substitution not death alone needed to be borne. It is indeed the wages of sin; but not, as some would have it, the *full* wages. So, if death be judgment, as for man it is, it is "*after* death *the* judgment;" which is not a repetition of the first death either, though it be the second: for the first death is *not* repeated. "It is appointed unto men ONCE to die, but after this the judgment."

The penalty borne by our Substitute, then, is something more than death. The *copher* must pitch the seams of the ark of salvation, that it may bring its freight of living souls in safely through the flood. Thus, and thus alone, is there perfect security, and the new scene is reached in peace. Salvation, as known and enjoyed here, if Scripture is to be at least our measure, does not stop short of this. Christ "gave Himself for our sins," says the apostle, "that He might deliver us out of this present evil world, according to the will of our God and Father." "Ye are not of the world," says the Saviour Himself, "even as I am not of the world." "If any man be in Christ," says the apostle again, "[καινὴ κτίσις] it is new creation: old things are passed away; behold, all things are become new."

For if Christ was our Substitute only upon the cross,—and this is true,—His identification with us does not and cannot cease there. We are *in* Him risen from the dead, and gone up to the glory of God. The manhood which He took up here He has taken in there. Nay, it is in resurrection, and only so, that He becomes "last Adam," as we have already seen, and as a "quickening Spirit," communicates that "more abundant life" of which He spoke, while yet on earth, to His disciples. (John x. 10.) As naturally we are children of the first man after his fall, and inherit from him its sorrowful results, even so as quickened of the last Adam, after the accomplishment of His work in our behalf, we are born into His status, and inherit the results in justification and acceptance with God, who "hath taken us into favor [$\dot{\varepsilon}\chi\alpha\rho\acute{\iota}\tau\omega\sigma\varepsilon\nu$] in the Beloved." (Eph. i. 6.) Already are we "seated together in the heavenly places *in* Christ Jesus."

We are thus past death and judgment. The Ark has brought us through. The old world, as that with which we are connected, is for faith already gone. In Him we are brought into a place of which the new world just emerged from its baptism was but the shadow; and here again we find a fresh aspect of atonement, and fresh results of it, in the *burnt*-offering, the *altar*, and God's covenant with creation.

If we have read God's words to Cain aright, Abel's offering was doubtless also a sin-offering. The distinct mention of the fat, as a thing apart, may go to prove this; for in the sin-offering, as afterward detailed, the fat was dealt with separately from the animal itself. It was, so to speak, the burnt-offering side of the sin-offering: for as the various sacrifices were but various aspects of the one great sacrifice, so there was in each some link of connection with the others, in witness of their common theme.

The development of these offerings as yet we do not find; still, so far as developed, if they be types or divine pictures of the great reality, we look for harmony among them, and shall assuredly find it from the very first. And in the order of application, which is the order observed here, the sin-offering comes naturally before the burnt-offering, to which now we come in Noah, in significant connection with the new place in which he appears.

For what is the burnt-offering? Literally, "the offering that ascends," or goes up to God. As we find here, it is what is sweet savor to Him; and though we shall find other offerings which are of sweet savor to God, as the meat and the peace-offering, yet is this the great and fundamental one. The term is inadequately given as "sweet savor:" it is properly, as in the margin, "savor of rest" or acquiescence, complacence. It thus unites with what is stated to be the purport of the burnt-offering, in a passage obscured by mistranslation in the common version. "He shall offer it of his own voluntary will" (Lev. i. 3.), should be rather, "He shall offer it *for his acceptance:*" and this is the key-note of the burnt-offering. In contrast with the sin-offering, which represents the solemn judgment of sin, it speaks of that perfect surrender of Christ to the will of God, tested and brought out by the cross, which brings out the supreme delight of the Father: "Therefore doth my Father love me, because I lay down my life, that I may take it again." That is the measure of our acceptance with God.

And to express this perfection in its manifold character it is that, we read, "Noah took of every clean beast, and of every clean fowl, and offered burnt-offerings on the altar." The burnt-offering was thus very frequently multiplied in a way that the sin-offering was not, and could not be. One sin-offering was ample for the putting away of sin, while to express the perfection of our acceptance with God, the burnt-offering is multiplied many times. Thus compare especially, in the twenty-ninth of Numbers, the sacrifices of the seven days of the feast of tabernacles; or those in Hezekiah's day (2 Chron. xxix.), or in Ezra's (ch. viii. 35.).

The presence of the altar too, for the first time, is full of meaning; for the altar is not of little significance in connection with the sacrifice. Our Lord Himself declares that "the altar sanctifieth the gift." We read of none in the case of Abel's offering, and in the fullest type of the Levitical sin-offering. (Lev. iv. 12, 21.) But what could sanctify the Lord's own gift? Certainly, nothing external. It was the perfection and dignity of His Person that gave value to His work, and the divine direction as to the altar afterward makes certain that it is Christ Himself who is before us in it. Thus fittingly from the sin-offering it is absent; for "He who knew no sin" being "made sin for us," the person is hidden, as it were, in what He represents, as the serpent of brass elsewhere conveys to us. On the contrary, in the type before us the altar necessarily finds its place. The dignity of His Person adds infinitely to the value of His work, and both together unite to lift us into the blessed place we have in Him. The ark and altar have thus a kindred meaning; and we find that atonement itself, necessarily getting its character from Him who makes it, does not restore man to his original place, but becomes the foundation and security of that new creation which the type here depicts, and with which God abides in unchangeable covenant.

The bow in the cloud, the token of this covenant with all that go out of the ark, I have elsewhere dwelt upon. It is typically the token of how God has been glorified (that is, *revealed*) in the work of the cross; His holiness, love, and truth banding the darkness of the most terrible storm of judgment ever seen. The storm passes, and the bow too to sight is gone, but faith finds its glories permanently enshrined in the jewels upon the foundations of the heavenly city, the pledge of its eternity. God is vindicated, satisfied, at rest; and where He rests, all things must needs abide too at rest.

## Chapter V.

*The Offering of Isaac. (Gen. xxii.)*

THERE were three men in Old-Testament times with whom it pleased God specially to connect Himself. To Moses He declares Himself as "Jehovah, God of your fathers, the God of Abraham, the God of Isaac, and the God of Jacob,"—and adds, "This is My name forever, and this is My memorial unto all generations." (Ex. iii. 15.)

Christians accordingly have been accustomed to trace in Isaac some of the lineaments of the Son of God, the Saviour. In Jacob, whose divinely given name is Israel, we may find no less, I believe, the Spirit of God; not personally, but in His work in man. While Abraham, at least in the memorable scene before us, (but elsewhere too, assuredly,) presents to us the Father. In His connection with these three men, then, God had already, ages before Christianity, foreshadowed its precious revelations.

In the history recorded in the twenty-second of Genesis, the apostle's words to the Galatians at least give us the *hint* of Isaac's presenting to us that greater Seed of Abraham, to whom God was in fact confirming His promise there. (Galatians iii. 17 should read, "*to* Christ.") And this is made clearer by what he states in Hebrews xi. 19—that Abraham received his son back, "in a figure," from the dead. It is in Christ risen from the dead that all nations of the earth shall be blessed indeed. This view of Isaac all his history confirms; but here is not the place to speak of it. Our purpose is to mark only what fresh features of atonement are given us in Isaac's offering, looked at as a type.

And here, the thing which we should first notice is, that here God Himself suggests a *human* offering. It has startled us all, I suppose, that He could do this; but we have only to connect it as a type with its antitype to see how gracious, in fact, this announcement was. Isaac did not, and was never meant to, suffer; but Another, in due time, was to take this place, and find no release from it, as he did. How the reality of what sacrifice pointed to bursts almost through the vail of figure here! Was it thus indeed that, as the Lord says, Abraham rejoiced to see His day; and saw it, and was glad? The bruised heel of the woman's Seed was in his mind assuredly. The Sufferer-Conqueror, acceptance by sacrifice, the blessing of all nations through his Seed, could but unite themselves with this suggested human offering, which was *not* Isaac, to give indeed a prospect full of joy, the deeper for its solemnity, to his believing heart.

The true Sacrifice was to be a human one, then. Man for men was to suffer and die; yet to be Conqueror in man's behalf over the serpent,—death only to Him the bruising of the heel. How this wrought in Abraham's mind we seem to see in what we know by the apostle's words was in it. A heel bruised is not fatal: death to the Conqueror here is not fatal. Isaac, the heir of the promises, must be offered up; and how then could these promises be fulfilled to him? *In resurrection,* answers faith, in Abraham's soul. "And he that had received the promises offered up his only begotten son, of whom it was said, that in Issac shall thy seed be called: accounting that God was able to raise him up even from the dead; from whence also he received him in a figure."

Only a figure, for Isaac does not really die: but if here is *figured* resurrection, it is the "Seed of the woman" surely (Abraham's true Seed also) that is to rise again; and *in resurrection* all promises are secured and fulfilled. Thus the Ark of salvation passes through the water-floods into the new scene of covenanted blessing, and thus *we* find our promised rest.

Is it strange to read, then, of Abraham and his immediate descendants, that "these all died in faith, not having received the promises, but having seen them afar off, and were persuaded of them, and embraced them, and confessed that they were strangers and pilgrims on the earth"?

But this offering of Isaac, seen in this manner, has a yet deeper significance. It is a father's offering of his son,—yea, as the apostle says, (for Ishmael has no place here,) of "his *only begotten* son." Here we can no longer speak of what Abraham's faith realized. For us, however, the type only becomes the clearer. If it is a man who offers himself, it is God who gives His only begotten Son. Isaac is here the example of perfect submission to the will of his father,—one with the will of God Himself. He but asks the question, as he bears the wood of the offering to the place of sacrifice, "Behold, here are the fire and the wood, but where is the lamb for a burnt-offering?" Abraham answers, "My son, God will provide Himself a lamb for a burnt-offering." And Isaac asks no more; but, in the vigor of his young manhood, silently surrenders himself, lamblike, to be bound and placed upon the altar. The voluntary character of the offering is here apparent, beyond what its being of the flock or herd implies.

But it is of the father that we think most. It is as Abraham's trial that Scripture presents it: "it came to pass that God did tempt Abraham." Point by point, the severity of the trial is brought out. "Take now thy son,—thine *only* son,—Isaac" (that is, "laughter:" for "Sarah said, 'God hath made me to laugh, so that all that hear it will laugh with me;'")—"whom thou lovest;—and get thee into the land of Moriah, and offer him there for a burnt-offering upon one of the mountains which I will tell thee of." He carries this three days in his breast, that it may be, not hasty impulse, but deliberate obedience. God knew His man; the man, too, knew his God. Promptly, "early in the morning," he starts, and in due time is there with unflagging steps, and faith in Him whom in his own body he has learned as "Quickener of the dead:" "I and the lad," he says to his young men, "will go yonder and worship, and *come again to you.*" All the while that he spoke so bravely, what was the strain on the father's heart? "Now I know," says He who understood it all,—"*Now I know* that thou fearest God; seeing thou hast not withheld thy son, thine only son, from Me."

But how wonderful to realize all this trial of a father's love in connection with a type of atonement! the pain and stress of it dwelt upon as if to make our human affections illustrate that amazing statement, that God "*spared not* His own Son, but delivered Him up for us all." What a proof of infinite love is here! The Seed of a woman, the Victor in the conflict with the serpent, the willing

Sacrifice for men's sins, is the Son of God sent of the Father to fulfill His will, and declare at once His holiness and His love. It is God Himself who in the manhood He has taken has acquired capacity to suffer and to die for man. He whose righteousness requires has Himself in love provided the atonement; humbling Himself to human weakness, suffering, and death. And we are not only brought to God in the value of so great a work, but know Him to whom we are brought as told out in the unspeakable gift of His Beloved, His only begotten Son.

Genesis thus, at the very beginning of Scripture, presents us with almost a full outline of the atoning work. Many are the important details yet to be filled in; but we have already certain fixed points which the fully developed doctrine will maintain and justify, not remove.

Atonement is by substitution; and in death, not life.

But death is the removal of the one who dies out of the sphere of his natural responsibility as a creature. Judgment is for the "deeds done in the body" only; if this also be borne substitutionally (and this is the "copher" of the ark: "atonement" which is something outside of and beyond death), then we are completely "covered;" sin completely removed from us before God.

But the substitution is not only of one perfect in the creature's place assumed, but infinitely more: it is the Eternal Son of the Father who, become man, makes this atonement. Hence the value of it is not to put us back into the old condition from which we fell, but to put us into a new condition altogether. The Second Man, risen from the dead, becomes the last Adam, Head of a new creation, fountain of life for His people in a new power and blessedness. Upon those, partakers of His eternal life, death (but no longer a penalty) may be in the meantime allowed to pass; only until the time of reconstruction, which shall make them fully what (as man) He is.

This is man's side of the atonement; but God is glorified in it,—His righteousness vindicated, His truth maintained, His love revealed. We are brought to God, know Him, and have our happy place as identified with the bright display of all He is. Good has indeed triumphed over evil, and it is the Seed of the woman who has bruised the serpent's head.

## Chapter VI.

*The Passover and the Sea. (Ex. xii. 14.)*

WE now come to the types of redemption, the recognized theme of the book of Exodus. That it is related to atonement in the most intimate way is evident; for if atonement is by blood, so is redemption. They are nevertheless different thoughts; and their difference, as well as their relation to each other needs to be considered.

Redemption implies purchase—price in some way paid, as the Greek words for it especially show;* although it is far removed from mere purchase, with which it is, in many minds, as in some creeds, confounded. Two things are implied beyond purchase: deliverance from alien possession, and that as an object of special interest to the redeemer. Even where the redemption is by power, as often in Scripture, it is implied that there is cost, if only of labor, effort, or peril incurred. We see at once that the first promise is a promise of redemption: the woman's Seed the Redeemer; the redemption itself by power from the serpent; the bruised heel the personal cost incurred. Yet this bruised heel, as has been shown, is, in another aspect of it, atonement; and the word *kopher*, in Hebrew, stands for both. The atonement *is* the ransom—the price of redemption.

The difference between the two thoughts is plainly this: that atonement has in view the divine

---

* Λύτρωσις and ἀπολύτρωσις, and the verb λυτρόω, all from λύτρον, a ransom-price; with ἐξαγοράζω, to buy out.

righteousness; redemption, the divine pity and love: atonement has respect to guilt; redemption, to degradation and misery. But the two connect here, that in the *provision* of atonement is seen the love of the Redeemer; in the *nature* of the ransom, the righteousness of the Judge, become thus the Justifier. Atonement and ransom are two different aspects of the same blessed work. Thus it is evident why the epistle to the Romans, which dwells on the reality of atonement, has for its key-note the *righteousness* of God; while we are "justified freely by His grace through the *redemption* that is in Christ Jesus." (Chap. iii. 24.)

In the book of redemption, then, we would expect to find atonement a central figure, as indeed we do; and yet *not* to find so much its intrinsic character dwelt upon as its delivering power for those in whose behalf it is accomplished;—that is to say, its manward rather than its Godward aspect. And this is how, exactly, the passover and the deliverance at the Red Sea present it to us. We must wait for Leviticus to realize in the sanctuary with God its full character for Him. Peace and deliverance must be first known and enjoyed before we are competent, and "at leisure from ourselves," to enjoy the manifestation.

Another thing that will help our apprehension of the types before us is to connect them with the epistle to the Romans, in which we find their real interpretation. Most evidently, the theme of Romans is the gospel salvation; and this also the types of Exodus show forth. In both, the deliverance is in two parts, or stages,—the first part having respect to the judgment of God; the second, to the bondage of one who reigns unto death. In the first, moreover, it is the blood that shelters; in the second, a passage through death (which the sea figures) by which we escape from the captivity in which we were enslaved.

The detail is of surpassing interest; and though a tale often told, it will bear retelling. Our present object requires the main points at least to be brought out, as we shall find in it a material development of the doctrine of atonement, as far as concerns its application to the need of the soul.

We must remember, as we consider them, that these are types of experience,—of realization and attainment,—as the salvation which the gospel brings is a known and enjoyed blessing, "the righteousness of God *revealed* to faith." The knowledge of shelter under the blood of the Lamb may long precede the knowledge of a new *ground* before God in Christ gone up from the dead to His place in the heavens. Blessed be God, the possession of the place does not depend upon the apprehension of it: it is ours before we *can* apprehend it to be ours. But let us remember, then, that we have here an order of apprehension which does not involve a corresponding order of possession.

Taking, now, Romans to interpret to us Exodus, Egypt is the world of nature, in which our standing is "in the flesh," and in which sin reigns over us unto death, as Pharaoh over Israel. It is a condition not realized as bondage until God works in the soul, but then an increasingly bitter one. Then the "law of sin" becomes a "law of death" also, and the soul groans for deliverance: this deliverance God's hand can alone accomplish.

And God's way is not as our way, nor His thought as our thought. *Our* way is, by the strength He gives, to deliver ourselves from the law of sin within us, and then to meet God, not as sinners, but as saints, and to find Him for us thus, accepting through Christ our imperfect obedience, and putting away our failures for His sake: *God's* way is to deliver us Himself, *not* by our own efforts blest of Him, but, *first*, meeting us as sinners and justifying us as ungodly by Christ's death for such.

Israel remain, subject to their old master, and not the first step taken of a walk with God, until they have learned that the judgment of God under which they lie in common with the Egyptians themselves is over, and they are safe,—saved by the blood of the lamb. The first passover is kept in Egypt, their journey not yet begun; but they eat it with girded loins and shod feet and ready staves, for that night they are to begin to go out.

They go out with judgment passed over and behind them; for us the wrath to come anticipated by faith and met in the cross, as we have already seen illustrated in the eight saved in the ark from the judgment of the flood. Israel start, "justified" instrumentally "by faith"—the faith by which they took refuge under the sheltered blood; "justified" effectively "by blood," which God saw, and passed over their houses. The blood declared the death inflicted upon the substitute: a penalty which in its very nature (as we have already seen) set the one for whom it was undergone outside the sphere of natural responsibility for evermore. Therefore says the apostle, "Much more, being now justified by His blood, we *shall be* saved from wrath through Him."

For the death threatened we here find plainly

judicial; a death which, if it end not the existence of the one under it, (as with man it does not,) involves in the shadow of it all that after-state. Such indeed had death been in its real nature, apart from the mercy of God from the beginning; yet in fact the first death on earth had been that of one pronounced righteous—"righteous Abel." Here, and in the flood, it was a death impossible to be confounded with this,—a strictly penal death. And this taken, the shadow of it also is removed.

This too the "blood" implies: blood shed, not in martyrdom, as Abel's, but by direct command of God, in exaction of penalty. How surely, then, "being now justified by His blood" insures our being "saved from wrath through Him"! All is settled,—completely, finally settled, according to the type here and the apostle's argument, when we begin to start on our path with God.

Settled forever Godward, but not yet are we outside the enemy's jurisdiction. But his power is apparently broken, and God Himself is with us. From this point, and before the sea is reached, "the Lord went before them by day in a pillar of a cloud, to lead them the way; and by night in a pillar of fire, to give them light; to go by day and night: He took not away the pillar of cloud by day, nor the pillar of fire by night, from before the people."

This complete settlement is given to their apprehension in the feeding upon the lamb within the house. It is such an obvious type, that it needs no insisting on. Death here, as had been permitted, significantly, since the flood, becomes the food of of life. But it is marked in this case, that the lamb must be, "not sodden in water," (or rather, boiled) "but roast with fire." Nothing must intervene between the fire and its object; even as with Christ made sin no perfection of His blessed life, no excellency of His person, could modify the full wrath-bearing due to the place He took. And it is the apprehension of this that perfects peace. It was not a commuted penalty that the blessed Lord bore, as is so largely now believed, but "our sins" in their just due. Such was the righteousness of God as set forth in the cross; and that righteousness therefore now requires and proclaims the justification of the sinner who trusts in it.

Thus we start, God for us and God with us, wholly and eternally, from the first moment of our start.

Of such questions, then, the experience at the sea is no reopening. The question is there between Israel and the power that had enslaved them; and if God come in, as He does and must, it is to show Himself openly in their behalf in the accomplishment of their deliverance.

And in the second part of Romans we find such a deliverance accomplished. The question here is no more Godward; it is, "O wretched man that I am! who shall deliver me from the body of this death?" The cause of this cry: "I see another law in my members, warring against the law of my mind, and bringing me into captivity to the law of sin which is in my members." The deliverance itself: "The law of the Spirit of life in Christ Jesus hath set me free from the law of sin and death." The ground of the deliverance: "Our old man is crucified with Christ, that the body of sin might be destroyed [or rather, *an-*

*nulled*], that henceforth we should not serve [be slaves to] sin."

In all this, we seem to have the Red-Sea passage before our eyes. Egypt, the territory of the flesh, is that within which the law of sin applies. The sea that shuts us in is death, the flesh's limit: beyond it, (only let us remember that we have in this type, not simple fact, but *realization* of the fact,) we are "not in the flesh."

Then, for deliverance, first, our own powerlessness must be realized, as with Israel, and in the seventh of Romans experience; then, that God's way for us is not by arming us with strength for conflict. Moses' rod is uplifted, and by the east wind (of sorrow) through the night (of the cross), the sea (of death) is smitten and divided from shore to shore. Thus we pass through death, untouched by it, are dead with Him—dead to sin, and, brought out the other side of death, are (consciously) in Christ what He is, and set free from the law of sin and death.

All this has been more fully told elsewhere. It is retold now to show how the cross meets and gives power over the corruption of the old nature, while as having life in Christ we are possessors of a new. The cross is our Pharaoh's overthrow, the condemnation of sin in the flesh, the end of all self-bettering, and our title to turn from self-occupation to occupy ourselves with Him in whom there is no condemnation, and to find that while "with open face we behold the glory of the Lord, we are changed into His image from glory to glory." This is the "law of the Spirit" that sets us free; and walking in the Spirit, we "shall not fulfill the lusts of the flesh."

# ATONEMENT.

But the passage through the sea does not land us in Canaan, as the doctrine of Romans does not put us in the heavenly places. We must for this add Joshua to Exodus, and Ephesians to Romans. We thus find that the passage through the flood has been divided into two for us, each part expanded and amplified, that we may the better view it. Here we pass over much of this, for our object is one precious truth, central indeed in doctrine, as the fact in divine history. May its contemplation grave it upon our hearts so as to enable us to say with the apostle, "God forbid that I should glory, save in the cross of our Lord Jesus Christ."

CHAPTER VII.

*The Tabernacle-Service.* (*Ex. xxv–xxx.*)

THE book of Exodus is divided manifestly into two parts, and that whether it be interpreted as type or letter. The first eighteen chapters treat thus of the deliverance of Israel from their old tyrant; the rest of the book, of their taking fully up the service of their Deliverer. In the typical view, to which the whole sacrificial system (with which we have now to do) essentially belongs, the first part gives us redemption *from* the slavery of sin; the second, redemption *to* God. The one is the complement of the other: the "service" of God is the only "perfect freedom."

We shall have yet to inquire as to the relation of the law to atonement; in what I propose just now, we have nothing to do with law *as such*. Typically, it becomes the symbol of that divine government to which as redeemed we are at once freely and necessarily subject. This is too much forgotten in interpretations of the book, and nothing seen except strict law—the ministration of death and of condemnation, as then it must be.

Typically, if the first part answer to the epistle to the Romans, the second answers (although much less completely) to the first epistle to the Corinthians. In it, the main feature is that habitation of God which Israel themselves are not but Christians are. This tabernacle and its services we have now to consider, so far as it develops new features of atonement, the central figure in all these types.

The new features that the tabernacle-service presents to us are the mercy-seat, upon which the blood is presented to God; the priest who offers the sacrifice; with the full completion of the altar of burnt-offering.

The mercy-seat, with the ark upon which it rests, is the throne of Him who has taken His place in the midst of His people. He is the God who dwelleth between the cherubim, and appears in the cloud upon the mercy-seat.

Christ is this mercy-seat, as the apostle in Romans iii. 25 declares; for the word "propitiation" there is the word so translated in Hebrews ix. 5, and that by which the Septuagint constantly renders the *capporeth* of the Old Testament. This Hebrew word is a noun derived from that intensive form of *caphar*, which is used commonly in the sense of atonement. Atonement is plainly stated to be made in the holiest on the day of atonement when alone the blood was actually brought in there and presented to God. And while shed actually for the sins of priest and people—the whole congregation of Israel,—it was declared to be made for the holy place itself, and for the whole "tabernacle of the congregation" (or "tent of meeting" rather, because there the people met with God). Afterward, atonement was made for the altar of burnt-offering by putting the same blood upon it. Thus the divine intercourse with men was sustained and justified. The sins of the people could not defile that upon which rested the precious blood of sacrifice. The *capporeth*, the seat of atonement, became indeed the *mercy-seat*,—the throne of righteousness a throne of grace. Toward the mercy-seat the faces of the cherubim, ever the symbols of judicial power, and thus connected with the throne, bent to behold the blood which proclaimed and satisfied the righteousness of God. All this in Israel was indeed but type and shadow: there was thus as yet no actual way of access into His presence. For us, the substance is come, and we have "boldness to enter into the holiest by the blood of Jesus, by a new and living way, which He hath consecrated for us, through the vail—that is to say, His flesh."

The apostle adds here the second thing which the tabernacle-service sets before us,—"A High-Priest over the house of God." (Heb. x. 21.)

The priest was the special minister of the tabernacle; the word in Hebrew signifying "minister." The apostle applies this in Hebrews viii. 1: "We have such a High-Priest, who is set on the right hand of the throne of the Majesty in the heavens; a Minister of the sanctuary, and of the true tabernacle, which the Lord pitched, and not man." The word used for "minister" here is *leitourgos*, one performing duties for the public good; and this completes the idea of the priest, as one serving in behalf of men in the sanctuary of God. Christ is thus "entered . . . into heaven itself, now to appear in the presence of God for us." (Ch. ix. 24.)

From Levi, third son of Israel, sprang both the Levite and the priest. This "third" speaks of resurrection, always connected with the third day\* (Comp. Hos. vi. 2.). And so the sign of the true

---

\*In beautiful connection with the spiritual significance of numerals, far too little thought of; for 3 is the number which speaks of divine fullness—of the Trinity, and thus of divine *manifestation;* as it is only when this is reached that, in Father, Son, and Spirit, God is fully revealed. But resurrection is that also which reveals God,—a work proper to Himself alone. (See Romans i. 4.)

priest (Num. xvii. 8.) was the dead rod blossoming and fruitful in the sanctuary. Levi's own name also, "joined," is full of meaning: it is the Mediator, in whose person and work God and man are really *joined*, who becomes the Priest.

If then in the tabernacle God's dwelling with man is foreshadowed, priest and mercy-seat are the necessary witnesses of how alone this can be.

His work of sacrifice accomplished, He Himself carries in the token of it into heaven, the place henceforth of His priestly ministration. By Him we draw nigh to God: His acceptance, who is our representative there, the measure of our acceptance. The high-priest thus represented the people. "In the presence of God for us" He who once died for us ever lives.

Access to God, no more afar off, but abiding with us,—access in the sanctuary of the heavens itself, and by One who represents us there: this is the new feature of the tabernacle-types as they speak to us to-day of the power and value of the blood of atonement.

But the altar also gets its full place and character. Indeed, while we find frequent mention of it in the book of Genesis, we have no description at all until we come to the second part of Exodus. The word in the Hebrew simply means "a place of sacrifice." The first command as to its construction we find in chapter xx. 24–26. This was to be the general construction which might have been adhered to, as some say, in the brazen altar, the frame-work of brass and wood being superimposed upon a substructure of earth.

"The altar sanctifieth the gift." If, then, the sacrifice represent the work of the Lord Jesus, it could not be sanctified by any thing outside. The person of the Offerer alone could give value to His offering. The character of the altar brings out and develops this.

The material, in chapter xx, is first of all, (and, as one might say, *preferentially*,) *earth:* "An altar of earth shalt thou make unto Me." We have evidently the thought of that which is fruitful. All fruit both Scripture and man's speech naturally call "fruits of the earth." But what is it that, in contrast with stone or sand, constitutes the fertility of earth? It is the readiness with which it suffers itself to be broken up into ever-finer particles; and to this its name in different languages seems to refer.* The spiritual application is readily made; and the yielding of the creature without resistance to the hand of God is that in which all real fruitfulness is found. In Him who gave Himself in manhood to know (in what other circumstances!) that path from which His creature had departed, Gethsemane and Calvary proved the perfection of His self-surrender. It was here the altar of earth symbolized Him: only one of many ways in which what was so precious to the Father is told out. "Therefore doth My Father love Me, because I lay down My life. . . . This commandment have I received of My Father."

The altar of *stone* is of course a different, and in some respects a contrasted thought. Stone is of the material of rock, the type of unyielding strength, a thought that we shall find repeated in the brazen altar, and linked there as here with

---

* Parkhurst gives *eretz*, "earth," from *ratz*, "breaking in pieces, crumbling;" χθων, from Heb. *kath*, "to pound, beat in pieces;" the Latin, *terra*, from *tero*, "to wear away;" and the Eng. *ground*, from *grind*.

that in which the secret of it is discovered. The Son of Man is the Ancient of Days. The rejected "Stone" is the "Rock of Ages." It is this that again gives value to the cross, and makes Christ the power of God unto salvation. Everlasting arms are they that are thrown around men. The human Sufferer is a divine Saviour.

It may seem to militate against this that Elijah builds his altar of twelve stones, expressly according to the number of the tribes of Israel; but this is no more against the interpretation I have given than it is against Matthew's application of Hosea's prophecy to Christ, that, according to the prophet himself, it is *Israel*, whom as a child God loved, and called His son out of Egypt. Whoever looks at Isaiah xlix. 3–6 will find how of necessity the place of the failed servant must be taken by One who cannot fail. *Substitution* may be as rightly stamped upon the altar as on the sacrifice; and this is surely the explanation here.

So the stone of the altar must not be hewn stone, nor must there be steps up to it. It is the intervention of God, not work or device of man. His attempt at this would only expose his shame: by any effort or contrivance he cannot rise above his own level. God could come down, and He alone exalt.

We come now to the brazen altar, where the brass covered a frame of shittim-wood, as in the ark, the table, and the altar of incense the gold covered it. In these, the two materials have been rightly held to speak of the two natures of our Lord: the shittim-wood, from a wilderness-tree, life conquering death, a growth not governed by its circumstances. Such was He who, growing up within the narrow circle of Judaism, ever spoke of Himself as "Son of *man;*" who, obedient to the law, breathed of divine grace; who was light shining out of darkness, life indeed, in the midst of death.

The gold I cannot conceive simply as "divine *righteousness;*" for who can conceive all the display of it in the tabernacle furniture speaking of nothing else but that? It is obvious, and often remarked, that it was characteristic of the sanctuary itself; and the sanctuary was the place where God manifested Himself; we having to consider it as with the vail rent, and the "first" tabernacle merged thus in the holiest of all. Moreover, in the things themselves there was this common character.* If the shittim-wood also represent the humanity of the Lord, the gold must needs represent, one would say, His divine: that by virtue of which alone He could manifest God in full reality. This it would be too narrow to limit to "righteousness," while of course this is contained in it. It is rather "glory," as the apostle calls the golden cherubim of the mercy-seat "the cherubim of glory." (Heb. ix. 5.)

In the altar of burnt-offering brass (or copper) replaces the gold, and for the same reason must surely represent the divine nature in our Lord, yet with an evident difference. It is not the type of divine manifestation, but of unchangeableness— endurance. It is constantly thus associated with iron, but which is a lower type, without the bright-

---

*"First, then, there are the things which are found in the Holy of holies and the holy place. The ark of the covenant, the table of the show-bread, and the candlestick with seven branches. This is what God had established for the manifestation of Himself within the house where His glory dwelt, where those who enter into His presence could have communion with Him."—(*Synopsis of the Books of the Bible.* Vol. I, p. 72.)

ness and sheen of the copper. In the successive degradation of the Gentile empires, the gold fades into silver, and the copper into iron. "Thy heaven that is over thy head shall be brass," Moses warns the people, "and the earth that is under thee shall be iron:" words that sufficiently illustrate both the similarity and the difference between these two things. Again, in the blessing of Asher, he says, "Thy shoes shall be iron and brass; and as thy days, so shall thy *strength* be." And the Lord even asks, in Jeremiah, "Shall iron break the northern iron and the steel [copper]?"

In connection with the altar of burnt-offering, this significance of the brass is of easy application. It was no mere creature-strength that was in Him upon whom rested the accomplishment of all the divine counsels of grace through the cross. "I have laid help upon One that is mighty" may indeed be said of Him. But how wondrous this character of endurance in Him who learns obedience through the things that He suffers: to whom it can be said, (His strength weakened in the way, and His days shortened,) "Of old hast Thou laid the foundations of the earth, and the heavens are the work of Thy hands" (Ps. cii. 25.)! Nay, the very power to stoop to such a place was the attribute of a nature necessarily divine.

And what does the brazen grate "beneath," "in the midst of the altar," speak but the deep capacity for suffering here implied? True, as, to be His type, the bird of heaven must die in the vessel of earth (Lev. xiv. 5.), so He must in the verity of manhood acquire capacity. The capacity is not thus to be measured by a mere human standard: **He was one blessed Person in whom Godhead and** manhood met; and in the depths of His being, as the grate within the altar, the fire of the cross could and did burn in abysses of nameless suffering to which no other sorrow could be like. To attempt to fathom or define would be presumption.

These, then, are features which the tabernacle-service adds to the idea of sacrifice. With this, we shall be prepared now better to come to that sanctuary-book, Leviticus, in which, in some sense finally, the whole heart of atonement is opened up to us.

## Chapter VIII.

### *The Burnt-Offering.* (*Lev. i.*)

THE theme of Leviticus is sanctification. Exodus closes with the tabernacle set up and the glory of the Lord filling the place of His habitation. Leviticus begins with the Lord speaking to Moses thence. His presence is in grace, but in holiness: "Holiness becometh Thine house, O Lord, forever." Holiness *in grace* is what sanctification implies.

First of all, then, as we open the book, we find given by God Himself the full details of those sacrifices which are the various aspects of that one Sacrifice in the power of which we are sanctified, or set apart to God. There are five, divided into two classes very distinct in character, according as they are or are not "sweet-savor offerings."

The term we have already had in connection with Noah's sacrifice. The burnt-offering, meat-offering (so called), and peace-offering are all said to be "for a sweet savor unto the Lord." The sin and trespass-offerings (which are quite distinct from one another moreover), are not that, although expressly guarded from disparagement, as "most holy." (Chap. vi. 17.) These last are indeed the special witnesses of divine holiness as against sin, while the former speaks more of the perfection of the offering on its own account. Judgment is God's strange act; in the self-surrender of One come to do His will in an obedience reaching to and tested by the death of the cross, God can have fullest and most emphatic delight.

It is evident that the burnt-offering has a very special place in the divinely appointed ritual of sacrifice. It not only comes first in order here, but in a certain sense is the basis of all the rest. The meat-offering is often spoken of as an appendage of it: "the burnt-offering and *its* meat-offering" (as Lev. xxiii. 13, 18; Num. xxviii. 28, 31; xxix. 3, 6, 9, etc.). The peace-offering is burnt upon it (Lev. iii. 3.). The altar, again, is especially styled "The altar of burnt-offering" (ch. iv. 7, 10, 18, 25, etc.); and on it, night and morning, the "continual" burnt-offering was offered: God would keep ever before Himself what was so precious to Him.

The very name of it speaks really of that: it is literally "the offering that ascends"—goes up to God. All the offerings did, of course; but of them all, this is *the* one that does: as of all the offerings consumed on the altar this is the only one that is entirely burnt,—the "*whole* burnt-offering." It is especially *God's* side of sacrifice, as (of the sweet-savor offerings) the peace-offering was *man's* side. Yet, on the other hand, it was *the* offering "for acceptance;" as that verse should read which we have in our common version as "He shall offer it of his own voluntary will." It should be, "He shall offer it for his acceptance." The measure of our acceptance is not simply that sin is put away: it is all the preciousness to God of that perfect "obedience unto death" by which sin is put away. This by itself would show us that the peculiar acceptability of sacrifice to God is what the burnt-offering expresses.

But this implies that voluntariness of character which, spite of the mistranslation already noticed, is clearly to be found in it. This attaches, indeed, to all the sweet-savor offerings, as it could not to the sin and trespass. But here the perfect self-surrender of Him who says, "Lo, I come to do Thy will, O God," is tested in the substitutionary victim-place. The offering is flayed and cut into [not pieces merely, but] *its* pieces: all is fully and orderly exposed. Then, head, fat, inwards, legs, the fire tries all, and sends all in sweet savor up to God.

This testing by fire we must carefully distinguish from what is by some confounded with it— the judgment due to sin. It has thus been said that while every offering did not set forth death, every one (as the meat-offering, and the similar offering of fine flour, permitted to the extremely poor for a sin-offering,) *did* set forth that of judgment. Older expositors have inferred from it that the Lord suffered for our sins *after* death. The whole thought is entire misconception, which would introduce confusion into the meaning of all the offerings. Consistency would then surely require that even the burning of the incense should typify judgment also; but who would not perceive the incongruity? The meat-offering would also be true atonement. The sin-offering burnt outside the camp and upon the ground, the true figure of judgment borne, would be indistinguishable from the burnt-offering here. The distinction between the sweet-savor offerings and the rest, carefully made in these chapters, could not be sustained; and judgment of sin would be declared a sweet smell to God. Moreover, the *answer* by fire, as on God's part the token of acceptance of the sacrifice, which we find again and again in the after-history, would connect strangely with the thought of judgment upon sin. In a word, if any thing is clear in these types almost, it is so that the altar-fire must have another meaning.

Now, it is admitted that fire is the common figure of judgment; yet when it is said, "The fire shall *try* every man's work, of what sort it is," we have another thought from that of wrath. "*Our* God is a consuming fire,"—not, surely, of wrath to those who can truly say, "Our God,"—but of holiness, yea, jealous holiness. It is this that implies of necessity His wrath against sin: it is no mere governmental display, but the result of His own nature—of what He in Himself is. But this holiness the Lord met indeed (as seen in all *sacrifice*) in the place of sin, and therefore of the wrath due to sin. All death—all blood shed in this way therefore was in atonement. Of the burnt-offering it is especially said, "It shall be accepted for him, to make *atonement* for him." And of all blood connected with the altar it is said, "I have given it upon the altar to make atonement for your souls, for it is the blood that maketh an atonement for the soul." (Lev. xvii. 11.) But while this is true of all sacrifice therefore, it is a very different thing to assert that judgment as *distinguished from* death is found in every offering, even where death was not and could not be. On the contrary, it may be maintained that death as the great public mark of divine judgment was what was kept prominently before the eyes of men in a dispensation which appealed to sight and sense, as all did more or less until the Christian. But then the judgment in this was not the judgment *after* death, but only the shadow of it: it was not judgment as *distinct* from death, surely. The *blood* was the atonement, so the law said; *not* the altar-fire which consumed the victim.

How different, the thought of wrath consuming its object, and of *holiness* exploring that which, exposed perfectly to its jealous searching, yielded nothing but sweet savor—"savor of rest"! Here the circumstances of the trial only enhance the perfection found. In human weakness and extremity, where divine power exposed, not sheltered, or sustained and capacitated for suffering, not rendered less; where upon One racked with bodily suffering fell the reproaches of those who in Him reproached God,—the taunts and mockings of heartless wickedness, taunting Him with His love; where the God whom He had known as none else, His all in the absolute dependence of a faith which realized human helplessness and necessity in all its terrors, in the utter loneliness and darkness from which all divine light had withdrawn:—there it was that the fire brought out nothing but sweet savor. Every part fully exposed and searched out,—"head, inwards, legs,"—mind and heart; spirit, soul, and all the issues of these in word and work and way,—all furnished that for God which abides perpetually before Him in unchanged and infinite delight. "Accepted in the Beloved," this delight it is in which we too abide.

Preceding the offering upon the altar was what was common to all these sacrifices—the laying of the offerer's hand upon the victim, and the necessary death and sprinkling of the blood. All these must be considered in their relation to the whole.

The "laying on of hands" we find in various connections both in the Old Testament and the New. It is given an important place in that sum-

ming up of the fundamental principles of Judaism,
—the "word of the *beginning* of Christ"\* (Heb. vi.
1, *marg.*)—from which the apostle exhorts the Hebrew converts to go on to "perfection"—the full
thing which Christianity alone declared. The
fundamental points or "foundation of Judaism he
declares to be such truths as "repentance from
dead works, and faith toward *God*, a resurrection
of the dead, and eternal judgment." Four central
and solemn truths these, but the real Christian
"foundation," Christ come and dead and risen, is
not among them. Consequently, as the apostle
urges throughout the epistle, there was in Judaism
no real "*purging of the conscience* from dead works,"
such as the blood of Christ gives, no perfecting of
the worshiper for the presence of God, and no way
of access into His presence. (Chap. ix, x.) What
then took the place of these for a believer, in the old
dispensation now passed away? In view of resurrection and eternal judgment, what had he to assure his soul? The words I omitted just now from
the statement of Jewish principles supply us with
the answer. He had "a teaching of baptisms,† and
of laying on of hands,"—of those baptisms, namely,
which in the ninth chapter (*v.* 10.) the apostle puts
in contrast with that work of Christ of which they
were indeed the shadow, and only the shadow. In
place of Christian assurance in the knowledge of

---

\* Not, as in the text, "the principles of the doctrine of Christ," which surely we could not be called to "leave."

† $\beta\alpha\pi\tau\iota\sigma\mu\tilde{\omega}\nu\ \delta\iota\delta\alpha\chi\tilde{\eta}\varsigma$,—"teaching," rather than "doctrine." The difference is, that "doctrine" would intimate that the explanation of the baptisms was given, which was not: Christianity alone gives the "doctrine," as the apostle does in chapter ix. Again, it is really "baptisms," as also in ix. 10,—not "washings," but ceremonial purifications, but not to be confounded either with Christian baptism, or even John's, which are always $\beta\alpha\pi\tau\iota\sigma\mu\alpha\tau\alpha$, not $\beta\alpha\pi\tau\iota\sigma\mu o\iota$.

the one completed work of atonement, he had forgiveness of individual sins by sacrifices continually needing repetition. How immense the difference! Out of which, alas! the enemy of souls has cheated the mass of Christians, replacing the "perfection," which God has declared, by sacramental absolutions, or repeated applications of the blood of Christ, —the old Jewish doctrine in a Christian dress.

Here, then, as a central part of Judaism, the "laying on of hands" had its place. It was the designation\* of the offering as the sacrificial substitute of him who offered it. Its importance lay in this, that it expressed thus the faith of the offerer for his own part. It said, "This is *my* offering." On the day of atonement, the high-priest in the same act said this for the people at large; but in these, each for himself said it. Faith must be this individual self-appropriating thing, although I do not mean by that what many would take from it, and what is taught by many.

When, in the vision of Zechariah the prophet, the high-priest Joshua, as the representative of guilty Israel, stood in filthy garments before the angel of the Lord, "He answered and spake unto those that stood before Him, saying, 'Take away his filthy garments from him.'" But that was not enough. "And unto *him* He said, 'Behold I have caused thine iniquity to pass from thee.'" (Chap. iii. 4.) How beautiful this direct assurance from God's own lips! translated, too, out of the lan-

---

\*The actual solemn appointment. The transferrence of sin was implied in these cases, just because it was a substitutionary victim that was marked out; but no transfer of any kind was *necessarily* shown in the act itself. I cannot enter upon the question of its meaning in the New Testament, which would lead me too far from what is before us. But I believe it every where expresses the same thing.

guage of type and figure into the plainest possible words, that it may be fully understood. Just so in every case for solid peace must there be this direct assurance to the soul. It is *God* who appropriates the work of Christ to us: not, indeed, in spoken words now, but in written ones. But when, then, does the Word of God thus appropriate Christ to us? This very scene may give the answer, It is when we *repent*.

Should I not rather say, "When we *believe*"? That would be quite true, of course. Surely it is true that he that believeth on Christ hath everlasting life. Yet there are those (and not a few) who stumble here, and say, "O yes, if I were sure that I believed!" And objectors urge, "Your faith that believers have eternal life Scripture justifies, but where is the word to say that *you* are a believer? This is your own thought merely, and you may be mistaken."

So I drop right down upon this: "Christ died for *sinners*." That surely is Scripture, and you will not say, I am not a sinner, or that I have not Scripture for that! Here, then, I have solid ground under my feet; here the everlasting arms hold me fast. And this is repentance, when I take home to myself the sentence of God upon myself, and thus join the company of lost ones, whom (in contrast with those "just persons who need no repentance") the Shepherd goes after till He finds and saves. Search as you will, you will find no other representative of the "sinner that repenteth" but the "sheep that was lost." (Luke xv.) To such lost ones, "clothed in filthy garments," the Lord says still, even by the mouth of Zechariah, "I have caused thine iniquity to pass from thee." Our appropriation here is but the apprehension of what He has done.

But if I urge "Christ died for sinners" in my own behalf, I have, as it were, my hands upon the head of the victim; and thus it is that my acceptance is declared to me. People confound this sometimes with what Isaiah says,—"The *Lord* hath laid on Him the iniquity of us all;" but the hand of the offerer could not by any possibility be *Jehovah's* hand. And I can, however long ago the precious Sacrifice has been offered, by faith consent to it as offered for me. Without this there can be no acceptance, no salvation. It is here that the position of the one who denies atonement is so unspeakably solemn.

The death of the victim follows at the offerer's hands: priestly work has not yet begun. "And he shall kill the bullock before the Lord." It is thus emphasized that the death of Christ was our act;* not as being morally one with those who slew Him, (although that is surely true, and most important in its place,) but by our sin necessitating His death on account of it: "the Son of Man *must* be lifted up." It is "before the Lord," as showing that the necessity on the other side was a divine one, proceeding from the holiness of the divine nature.

Thus the "blood that maketh atonement for the soul" is now provided. "And the priests, Aaron's sons, shall bring the blood, and sprinkle the blood round about upon the altar that is by the door of the tent of meeting." This sprinkling of the blood

---

*I cannot see that the offerer here represents Christ, and therefore as laying down His own life. It seems an unsuited act to represent this. The offerer when laying on his hands on the victim just before cannot represent Him, moreover; nor where he offers "for his acceptance."

is in testimony of the work accomplished, and for the eye of God, as much as that passover-blood of which He declared, "When I see the blood, I will pass over you." If the blood it is that maketh atonement for the soul, that blood is of necessity presented *to God*, as the atonement was made to Him. It is not here put upon the person, and we have not yet got to consider that; but wherever put, the blood is for God. And indeed it is the assurance of that which gives it power, as the apostle says in Hebrews, to "purge the conscience from dead works to serve [or "worship"] the living God." Thus "the *heart* is sprinkled from an evil conscience." (Chap. ix. 14; x. 22.) It is faith's apprehension of the efficacy of that perfect work.

After the blood-sprinkling comes the flaying of the offering, the skin of which, as we learn afterward (ch. vii. 8), belongs to the priest that offers it. Christ is evidently the One typified by this sacrificing priest, and so we learn whose hand it is bestows that by which the shame of our nakedness is forever put away. It is the skin of the *burnt*-offering, not the *sin*-offering. It is not true that Christ's death merely puts away our sins: it furnishes (though not alone, as we may see hereafter,) the "best robe" for the Father's house. "Raised up from the dead by the glory of the Father," the place which as man He takes is the divine estimate of that "obedience unto death" of which He says, "Therefore doth My Father love Me, because I lay down my life that I might take it again. No man taketh it from Me, but I lay it down of Myself. I have power to lay it down, and I have power to take it again. This commandment have I received of My Father." (Jno. x. 17, 18.) This is the true burnt-offering aspect of the cross—the full sweet savor. But the place He takes as man He takes for men. This gives us the measure of our acceptance in the Beloved, by which our nakedness is indeed covered, and its shame removed.

The burnt-offering having been flayed, is divided into its parts; all exposed to the light of heaven, then to the altar-flame. The word for burning even is not the word for ordinary burning, but for fuming as with incense: all goes up, not as the smoke of judgment, but as pure sweet savor.

It remains but to speak of the grades of the burnt-offering, and with this of the different animals that are used. Of these the bullock, the highest, without doubt is the type of the laborer for God (1 Cor. ix. 9, 10.): Christ was the perfect Servant, the character in which Isaiah liii. especially presented Him.

The sheep speaks of meek surrender to the divine will, a more negative thought in some sense; yet it is the "*Lamb* of God that taketh away the sin of the world." Here too it is the *male* sheep, which gives the more positive character of devotedness, as appears in the "ram of consecration," in the eighth chapter.

The goat is the type of the Sin-bearer as such, as our Lord's classification of sheep and goats would surely intimate. Hence it is the sin-offering for the ruler and common Israelite as well as for the whole nation on the day of atonement.

The turtle-dove and pigeon, birds of heaven both, naturally represent the Lord as come from thence. The type is brought out in great distinctness where in the cleansing of the leper the bird offered dies in a vessel of *earth* over running (living) water: a precious figure of that humanity full of the Spirit in which a Divine Being gained capacity to suffer.

The dove is the bird of love and sorrow: most suited associations of thought with a heavenly stranger whom love to God and man has brought into a world of sin. The pigeon—the *rock*-pigeon, with its nest (like the coney) there,—is as suited a thought of One come down to a strange path of faith.

All these are blessed types of our Lord in various perfections. They are connected with higher or lower grades of offering, not as in themselves of necessity conveying higher or lower thoughts. The lowest grade here is that of the birds, surely not the lowest thought of Christ's person,—rather the contrary. The reason is one which can be easily understood. Does not the very glory of His Godhead prevent many realizing the perfection of His manhood? Do not many bring in the thought of the "bird," as it were, without the "vessel of earth" in which alone it could die? And the changes in the ritual here are quite accordant with this. The bird is not divided to the same extent as the bullock or the sheep: the internal perfection is not in the same way seen. There is little blood, too, for the altar; and *there is no skin for the priest*.* Is it not the necessary result where the Lord's manhood is dimly realized? Thank God that this is still a sweet-savor offering to Him! What He finds in Christ is not measured by what we find, nor our acceptance by our apprehension of it. And these lower grades bring out *our* thoughts. Still we lose by their poverty. May He graciously bring His beloved people, even here, more to the knowledge of His own.

---

* The *feathers* are not rejected, as in our version: the margin is better.

## Chapter IX.

### *The Peace-Offering.*

AS the burnt-offering gives especially the divine side of the work of Christ, so the peace-offering dwells rather upon its effects with regard to men. This must not be taken in too absolute a way as respects either. The burnt-offering is for man, of course, and in atonement; and the skin removed undoubtedly carries us back to the coats of skins which clothed our first parents, as we have already seen. On the other hand, in the peace-offering, who could forget the Father's joy in that which brings the prodigal to the Father's table? And this is what the peace-offering presents to us. Still this "peace" is what the offering effects for man with God. It is rather an effect of the work which is contemplated than a new aspect of the work itself.

For this reason we have necessarily, in connection with our present subject, less to do with it. The main peculiarities connect with the necessary distinction of destination of the offering, of which only the fat is burnt upon the altar, while the rest of the animal belongs either to the priest or to the offerer himself,—the only sacrifice in which the offerer does partake. In the lower grades of the sin-offering the priest has his part; the offerer no where but in this. Here, then, the peace-offering fulfills its name, and finds most evidently its distinctive character.

The peace-offering may be of the herd or flock,

male or female, bullock or sheep or goat. Birds are omitted, with a manifest propriety, which confirms fully the meaning ascribed to them. "The bread from heaven," as the Lord says in the gospel, is what "the Son of *Man* shall give you." If we speak of communion, which we have seen to be the point here, it must be the Son of Man, sealed of the Father, that must be the basis of it. True, if He were not God over all blessed forever, all the preciousness would be lost for us. Nevertheless it is in His manhood that we apprehend Him doing that work which alone brings us to God. Even in the burnt-offering we see that the bird, though a higher thought, comes in necessarily as a lower grade. Here it disappears. It is in the joy brought out of sorrow that I find what establishes my soul in peace with God. It is the value of His manhood's work in which I draw near, although none but such as He was could have had power to lay down His life and again to take it.

In the peace-offering and sin-offering alone is the female permitted,—in the latter indeed enjoined, although only in the lower grades. It seems clear that it gives thus the character of comparative feebleness or passiveness to the offering, but it is not clear that that is all we are to gather from it. We have seen that the lower grades of sacrifice represent in general thoughts true in their place, but here *mis*placed. Yet in Numbers xix, the female is commanded where there is no other grade at all. Here, it is surely impossible that mere feebleness can be intended. Passiveness may indeed have its suited place with reference to the sin-offering, but here, and in the peace-offering also, the type of the sheep seems by itself to represent this; and in the sin-offering, the sheep is expressly to be a female too. Taking all these together, I have little doubt that those are right who believe the female to be the type of fruitfulness, which in connection with the thought of passiveness or quiet subjection to suffering seems here not out of place, but eminently in place. Is it not true, as there are in man and woman characters which complete each other, and give, as thus seen together, perfection to the divine idea of man, so in our Lord, as the perfection of all human excellency, the male and female characters find both their place?

Jehovah's Servant, in the accomplishment of those counsels of love and wisdom which were laid upon Him, giving up His life in meek surrender, even to that cross in which the full due of sin was His to meet and put away for us forever: —these things seem fitly to unite here to give the complete character to the peace-offering. They may seem to connect with other offerings, as the goat especially with the sin-offering, but they seem all rightly to meet and give character to this central sacrifice, where in a common joy Blesser and blessed, Saviour and saved, God and man, stand. Thus we find here no *grades* really, as in the burnt-offering we have found, and in the sin-offering shall much more find them. Here, the details of the sacrifice, whether for cattle, or sheep, or goat, seem almost absolutely the same.

The details are such as we have already sought to trace the significance of. The animal is presented to Jehovah, designated as the substitute of him who offers it, killed, and the blood sprinkled on the altar round about. Then all the fat is put upon the altar, *upon the burnt-offering*, which is on the wood that is on the fire; and it is emphatically pronounced a sweet-savor offering.

That which I have emphasized is very precious. Our communion is founded upon nothing less than the full acceptance of the beloved Son of God,—acceptance in all the perfection which we have already seen the burnt-offering expresses. This gives the measure of communion as God intends it; the measure of our apprehension is quite another thing.

## Chapter X.

### *The Sin-Offering.* (*Lev. iv.–v.* 13.)

WE now come to a class of offerings distinguished broadly from those classed as "sweet-savor," by the fact of their being in no wise voluntary, but the specific requirement for actual sin. The burnt-offering and peace-offering both clearly recognized, of course, the condition of men as sinners. Apart from this, they had indeed no meaning. But in no case are these offered for specific acts of sin. In their case we find, "If any man of you bring an offering unto the Lord;" in those now before us, "If a soul shall *sin*, he shall bring his offering."

The sin and trespass-offerings both speak of the judgment of sin, that judgment which is indeed no sweet savor to God, but His "strange work,"—not the delight of His love, but the necessity of His holiness. The sin-offering deals with sin in view of the divine *nature;* the trespass-offering, in view of the divine *government*. The words "sin" and "trespass" well convey this difference, the thought of restitution having a prominent place in the trespass-offering, as the sin-offering alone exhibits that necessary separation of God from sin which is at once the necessity of His nature, and its most awful punishment.

Yet it is striking that this, the most essential and characteristic feature, is only in fact found here in the sin-offering for the priest and for the congregation of Israel. In these cases alone do we read of the victim being burned without the camp, not upon the altar, the consecrated place, but in the outside place of the leper and unclean. It is to this the apostle refers in the last chapter of Hebrews, where he points out the absolute necessity of the Lord's taking such a place as is typified here in order to any true atonement: "For the bodies of those beasts whose blood is brought into the sanctuary by the high-priest for sin are burned without the camp. Wherefore Jesus also, that He might sanctify the people with His own blood, suffered without the gate." It is a striking thing indeed that, of all the various sacrifices offered by the law, no blood but that of a sacrifice such as this should have power to penetrate into the sanctuary at all. The burnt-offering spoke of that which to God was precious beyond all else, but the blood was simply sprinkled round about upon the altar: the peace-offering spoke, according to its name, of peace made with God, and communion established between God and man, but here also the blood was only sprinkled on the altar round about; nay, there were various forms of the sin-offering itself where the effect was plainly stated to be to "make atonement for his sin" who brought it, but where, the body of the beast not being burned without the camp, the blood at the most anointed the horns of the altar of burnt-offering. Only in two cases, as I have already said, among the seven that are specified here, is that done in which alone lies the essence of true atonement.

This shows clearly in what manner we are to regard these other forms, namely, as lower grades, or less complete views of what only in its full completeness could satisfy God. In the lowest, indeed, they are plainly said to be provisions for the poverty of the offerer: "if he be not able to bring a lamb,"—"if he be not able to bring two turtle-doves." In the case of the ruler, and in the first case of "one of the common people"—both, of course, on the footing of the Israelite simply,—it is or should be clear that they neither of them represent the place or the knowledge of the Christian; yet they are most instructive to us as enabling us to see just what is and what is not dependent upon clearness of knowledge upon a theme so all-important as is this. However, it will be all no doubt plainer as we look at the details of the type before us.

The first case, then, is that of the "anointed priest," clearly the *high*-priest, he who represents the whole people before God, the well-known figure of Christ Himself. Typically, this seems a departure from the usual order, for the offerer in other cases seems *not* to represent Christ, and this change must have a meaning. Naturally, we think of the day of atonement, where Aaron and his sons are distinguished in their offering from the people of Israel, and where we as Christians are represented in Aaron's house. In the offering of Leviticus iv, the high-priest stands alone; but the next offering, parallel in every particular to this one, is for the "whole congregation of Israel,"—those manifestly whom the high-priest represents: in the application must we not say, the Church? It is evident that this gives us two classes on essentially different footing,—those for whom the sanctuary is opened, and those who while accepted are outside worshipers.

But why, then, is Christ here first of all by Himself, and the people apart, and not rather, as in the day of atonement, the high-priest and his house, or

Christ and His people together? It seems to me to bring out representation more clearly, but especially, as I think, makes way for a comparison with the two next offerings, where the ruler and one of the common people take the place of the priest and congregation, and the character of the whole is lowered.

The literal application supposes the sin of the high-priest himself, and his place as such secured, his incense altar anointed with the blood of the sin-offering. As a type, it is Christ confessing the sin of His people, and the place which through His offering He takes before God, He takes for them, and they in Him. Thus for the people the blood in the same way is sprinkled before the vail, and anoints the golden altar of incense.

It is here only that we find, as already stated, the burning of the victim without the camp, upon the ground also and not upon the altar. It is thus Christ made sin for us—not seen in the perfection of His person as in the burnt-offering, but identified with those for whom He had undertaken. No where but in this outside place could He reach the objects of His grace to bring them up out of the horrible pit and out of the miry clay in which they were hopelessly ingulfed, and in which alone His feet could find footing. How important, then, to have a right apprehension of this essential feature of His wondrous work! Yet there are those among evangelical Christians so called who see no difference between the Lord's sufferings in life and those in His death,—between Gethsemane with its bloody sweat and the blood of the cross! They see not the contrast between a time of which He yet says, "I am not alone, for My Father is with

Me" and that of His cry, "My God, My God, why hast Thou forsaken Me?" The three hours' darkness while He hangs upon the tree is almost universally misinterpreted as the sympathy of Nature with her Head and Lord, whereas it is the manifest expression of the withdrawal of Him who is light, and finds, therefore, its true interpretation in that cry of forsaken sorrow.

We come, then, here for the first time to the full and undeniable type of wrath borne, and needed to be borne in order to atonement. The *copher* of the ark had hinted, as we have seen, at such necessity; but it only hinted. Now, the truth was plainly set forth. Every sacrifice had shown, what is announced as a principle a little later, that, as the apostle says, "without shedding of blood is no remission." But here we see *what* blood alone could meet the atonement of righteousness upon the sinner. Not death merely, but death and after this the judgment, is man's doom. The full reality of sacrifice, of which each separate sacrifice was but a fragment, must meet both parts of this. The cross as death and as curse did this.

But how beautiful to see even in the sin-offering the type preserved of that inward perfection which was necessarily and ever God's delight and the basis of all the acceptability of it. Only He *could* be "made sin for us" who Himself "knew no sin." Accordingly the fat here, as in the case of the peace-offering, is put upon the altar, and in the case of one of the common people it is even said to be for a sweet savor. While this is not said with regard to the first two cases, the word used for the burning on the altar is the ordinary one for that, different from that employed for the burning of the victim on the ground outside the camp.

Wrath endured, the due of sin in its full measure reached, God can open the sanctuary, and give a place in His presence where in the complete security of the seven-times-sprinkled blood we can stand in unquestioned nearness, and the heart pour itself out in praise, the blood anointing the incense altar. For us the vail is rent, as we know, but as we do not find in the type before us: *we* have boldness to enter into the holiest itself.

Thus far the divine thought, the perfection of the offering. In the next two cases the whole character of it is lowered. We have now the ruler and one of the common people taking the place of the high-priest and congregation in the former two; the burning outside the camp is no longer found; and the blood of course does not enter the sanctuary at all, but is first put upon the horns of the altar of burnt-offering, and then poured out at the bottom of the altar.

All this speaks evidently of a lower grade. Whatever may be the difference of the offerer, and although this might account for the blood not being brought into the holy place, the apostle's words link these rather with the body of the victim not being burned without the camp; and of the absence of this who can find a reason thus? For the least as for the greatest atonement must be the same. It is clear, therefore, that we have in this only the sign of the commencement of a descending scale of offerings, in which we find the poverty and confusion of man's thoughts allowed to have their place, in order that on the one hand we may realize the consequence of falling short in the apprehension of divine grace, while on the other we learn that that grace will still manifest itself as such, and that God's actual acceptance of us is not measured, after all, by our apprehension of it, but by His own estimate of the value of the work of His beloved Son.

The goat here still speaks of substitution, of Christ in the sinner's place, for the Lord's own use of it, as contrasted with the sheep in the picture in Matthew xxv, assures us fully of this. But while seen as a substitute thus, what substitution implies and necessitates is not seen. The sin is none the less forgiven, but the offerer remains an outside worshiper merely. Christ is for him a "ruler" in the heavens, not a representative proper, as the priest is. He remains, as people say, "at the foot of the cross;" does not see that through the work of the cross Christ has entered heaven, and taken a place before God in which he as a believer stands. This is, alas! where the mass of so-called evangelical systems leave their adherents,—the Jewish place, clearly, for the standing of one of the common people of Israel is not even a type of ourselves. We are, as the apostle tells us, "a spiritual house, a holy priesthood, to offer up spiritual sacrifices, acceptable to God by Jesus Christ." We therefore are brought nigh, and belong to the sanctuary as did Aaron's house,—with the unspeakable difference here also of the vail being rent: "Therefore," says another apostle, "having boldness to enter into the holiest by the blood of Jesus, by a new and living way, which He hath consecrated for us through the vail, that is to say, His flesh; and having a High-Priest over the house of God; let us draw near with a true heart, in full assurance of faith."

For the goat a lamb might be offered, and here we see again how a type higher in itself may give from its connection a lower because a less congruous thought. The latter speaks, as we know, of the personal perfection of Christ, but here it displaces the goat, so that the thought of real substitution is fading away: the ritual of the offering is otherwise the same.

In the next cases, however, the ritual itself is changed; for now we find first the trespass-offering (which is nearest to the sin-offering), and then the burnt, and finally even the meat-offering introduced. The inability of the offerer is now, moreover, more distinctly recognized. It is plain, therefore, that the mention of the trespass-offering in this place does not imply, as some have imagined, that there is no essential difference between it and the sin-offering, or else it would prove the same for the others mentioned. There is a very marked and unmistakable difference. It is distinctly "his trespass-offering for his sin which he hath sinned . . . for a sin-offering." Even as a trespass-offering it has not its full character: it is a "lamb, or a kid of the goats," not a ram. I do not doubt that here we have the case of those who look at atonement as a mere provision of divine government instead of a necessity of the divine nature. It is one truth substituted for another, the less deep for the deeper; but of all this we shall have a more fitting place to speak.

The substitution of the burnt-offering, or its introduction rather into the ritual of the sin-offering, is remarkable, as it is distinctly a provision for poverty: "if his hand cannot reach to the sufficiency of a lamb;" and, moreover, the sin is called a "trespass," while here, again, the two turtle-doves or two young pigeons speak of what is highest in itself, lowest because of its incongruity, in fact the lowest type of the burnt-offering, as we have seen; for a sin-offering most incongruous of all.

Lastly, if he be not able to attain to this, even a meat-offering of fine flour is permitted, and here, although no blood at all is shed, it is distinctly offered and accepted as a sin-offering, and his sin is forgiven him just as before. How clearly and beautifully does the grace of God shine out in all this! If it be Christ trusted in in view of sin, God knows the nature and sufficiency of His blessed work, and reckons the value of that work to the offerer, unknown though to him it be. It is a point which if seen aright will deliver us from much narrowness, and comfort us with the largeness of the grace of God.

It is evident to me that sin in the nature as much as in the act is dealt with in the sin-offering. We must not be misled as to this by the consideration that it is only for actual sins that it is offered. The fruit manifests the tree, and it is in this sacrifice alone that we find the judgment of God taking effect upon the whole victim. The burnt-offering, although wholly burnt, does not in this give the type of wrath or condemnation, as we have seen, but the very opposite. The very word for the burning is different; it is sweet savor and nothing else. Here, on the contrary, judgment has its full course. This complete judgment of nature and practice alike is absolutely necessary, in order that the blood of propitiation may be able to enter the sanctuary.

## Chapter XI.

### *The Trespass-Offering.*

THE trespass-offering is for sin looked at as injury, and in view of the *government* of God, as the sin-offering contemplates it in its intrinsic character as abhorrent to His *nature*. Thus restitution—"amends for the harm that he hath done"—is so prominent a feature in the trespass-offering, the ram of which is itself valued, and becomes part of the repayment. The governmental view of the atonement, which so many in the present day contend for, while it is thus justified as a partial view, falls entirely short in its estimate of it when taken as the *whole*. It is not in *government* merely that God hides His face from sin. The darkness and the cry of desertion of the cross express more than governmental atonement. Indeed, to the mass of writers upon the subject these are features whose significance is of little import. In the punishment of the wicked finally, few or many stripes express the governmental award of the "great white throne;" but the "utter darkness," the necessary separation of God from what is abhorrent to His nature, is not merely governmental, but the necessary portion alike of all.

Hence that offering burnt in the outer place alone had power to penetrate into the sanctuary, the abode of divine light, and when really offered, to rend the vail and bring us into the light of the divine presence. Hence, as we have seen, the sin-offering for the high-priest and congregation

## ATONEMENT.

is the only one which we can regard as the true sin-offering. All others were but partial and defective forms.

The trespass-offering, as far as its ritual is concerned, has little to distinguish it from these lower grades of the sin-offering. There is no laying on of hands, so far as we read, and the blood is not put upon the horns of the altar, but simply sprinkled on it round about. The fat alone is burnt upon the altar; the rest eaten by the priests.

The ram is the victim here alone appointed, although elsewhere for the leper (ch. 14) and the Nazarite (Num. vi.) a lamb was to be offered. The ram was evidently the fuller type,—the female sheep and lamb giving the character of meek submission, the male sheep more of energy in devotedness; in the coverings of the tabernacle the ram-skins were dyed red, to show that devotedness even to death which characterized the Lord.

The great thought impressed upon us in the trespass-offering is that of restitution—amends for the harm done. This has to be estimated by the priest in shekels of silver after the shekel of the sanctuary. The estimation was to be a divine one, the priest giving the divine judgment; while the restitution-money was to be also the sanctuary shekel. But even this was not enough; the fifth part more was still to be added; for God would have an overplus of good result from evil, not mere making up to where things were before. That would not be worthy of Him. How could He have suffered sin at all, merely to show His power in vanquishing it and no more? Such victory would be little better than defeat. And yet this is what the mass of Christians perhaps suppose.

Christ is to bring us back, they think, to the point from which Adam wandered, or which he ought to have reached but failed. But this is a deep degradation of Christ's blessed work. On the contrary, it is a second Man and a new creation which the word proclaims, of which the old is but the mere figure, and to which it gives place. The "fifth part more," heartily believed, would do away with much error and replace it with much precious and needed truth.

Christ has restored that which He took not away; but it is after the divine and not the human fashion. As the trespass-offering is here looked at in connection with trespasses against God or against man, so the cross has brought to God an infinite glory overpassing all the dishonor done to Him by the fall of the creature, and to man a wealth of blessing such as Eden never knew.

For the detail of this we must go to the New Testament. The trespass-offering itself says nothing even in type, only indicates an over-recompense, the nature of which it does not further declare. But we, thank God, can declare it. "Now," says the Lord, speaking of what He was soon to suffer,—"Now is the Son of Man glorified, and God is glorified in Him; if God be glorified in Him, God shall also glorify Him in Himself, and shall straightway glorify Him." (Jno. xiii. 31, 32.) This surely is the key of all that the offering implies. The glory of God accomplished by One who has become Son of Man for this purpose; this answered in glory by God, an answer in which the objects of His grace are made to share: how far beyond the mere putting away of sin and its results is thus indicated! Goodness, holiness, righteousness in God maintained and manifested as no where else; mercy and grace declared how wondrously! For men, in result, not an earthly paradise again restored, but heaven opened; not innocence, but the image of God in righteousness and holiness of truth; not Adam-life, but Christ as Life eternal; not part with merely sinless men, but part with Christ in glory. For "not as the offense even so is the free gift; . . . . for if through one man's offense death reigned by one, much more they which receive abundance of grace and of the gift of righteousness shall reign in life by One, Jesus Christ."

Thus in both ways through our Trespass-Offering is the fifth part more made good. And now, having completed, briefly enough, our survey of these Levitical sacrifices, let us look back at them for a moment in what was in fact, as we see in the law of the leper, the order of application. This was not a simple reversal of the order in which these chapters give them however, for while the trespass-offering preceded in this way all the rest, and the sin-offering always, for an obvious reason, the sweet-savor offerings, on the contrary the burnt-offering invariably preceded the rest of these; the meat-offering following next, and connected with it often as if its proper appendage,— "the burnt-offering and *its* meat-offering" (Lev. xxiii. 13, 18; Num. viii. 8; xv. 24; xxix. 3, 9, etc.) the peace-offering closing the whole. When, however, the peace-offering alone was offered, the meat-offering became its adjunct, and was prescribed in a scale proportionate to the value of this, as it was in the case of the burnt-offering itself (Num. xv. 1-14).

First, then, we have the offerings which settled the whole question of sin as against the offerer, and then those for acceptance, or a sweet savor. Not only the burnt-offering was for the "acceptance" of him who brought it, but the peace-offering also (Lev. xix. 5; xxii. 25). This is not said directly of the meat-offering, but it is of the sheaf of first-fruits (Lev. xxiii. 11), with which, however, a burnt-offering was offered. The difference of course results from the meat-offering being no real sacrifice, although it might be offered, as we have seen, even for a sin-offering, where the extreme poverty of the offerer permitted nothing more. The meat-offering spoke of Christ, but in the perfection of His holy life, not as a vicarious Substitute for sinners. The perfection of His life could not, it is plain, atone for sin, nor be in itself the acceptance of a sinner; yet it could not be omitted either from God's estimate of the work of His beloved Son. Hence, as it makes necessary part of that accomplished righteousness in the value of which He has entered into His presence and as man sat down there, so in its value also we stand before God. The place of the meat-offering in connection with the burnt-offering speaks clearly here.

Finally, the peace-offering closing all is witness to us that God would have our communion with Himself find its measure and character from the apprehension of this place of acceptance and what has procured it for us: in Christ; as Christ; justified and sanctified in His precious name. When we compare this place with the feebleness of our apprehension of it, we have cause indeed for the deepest humiliation before God; but what reason for encouragement also in this grace that continually beckons us forward to enjoy our portion according to the fullness of it as the word of God's grace so constantly presents it before our eyes, and in the power of the Spirit of Christ given to us, without limit, save as, alas! unbelief on our part may impose a limit!

## Chapter XII.

### *The Two Birds.* (*Lev. xiv.* 1–7; 49–53.)

FOR our purpose, it would be evidently a diversion to take up the various *applications* of the sacrifices which we find in the book of Leviticus or elsewhere; but where we find variation in the sacrifice itself, we may expect a development of new features in that one great offering which all these foreshadow. Such variation we have in that which is enjoined for the cleansing of a leprosy which was already healed; and if we passed it over, we should manifestly miss designed instruction as to the work of atonement.

Here, "two birds, alive and clean," are to be taken, one only of which is to be killed, and this in a remarkable way, namely, "in an earthen vessel, over running [literally, living] water." "As for the living bird," it is added, "he [the priest] shall take it and the cedar-wood and the scarlet and the hyssop, and shall dip them and the living bird in the blood of the bird that was killed over the living water; and he shall sprinkle upon him that is to be cleansed from the leprosy seven times, and shall pronounce him clean, and shall let the living bird loose into the open field." In the cleansing of the leprous house, the same thing precisely is enjoined.

We have already, in the burnt-offering and sin-offering both, become familiar with the type of the bird. In the case before us there are, however, some notable differences from these, which all tend to show that here we have the type in its fullest character,—the *most* typical of all its forms. Thus it is neither dove nor pigeon nor any particular species that is prescribed, but simply two "birds." It is the bird as such, irrespective of specific qualities,—"the bird of *heaven*," according to the constant phraseology of Scripture,* a being not of earth. Its dying in a vessel of earth, by its plainly designed contrast, only brings out the more this character, and is interpreted for us by the apostle's application of the figure (2 Cor. iv. 7) so as to render mistake impossible.

Again, while the bird-type, in the sin-offering plainly, and in the burnt-offering no less really, is as a misplaced higher thought, in fact a lower one, —here, on the other hand, it is the manifestly divine one, remarkable as being defined neither as sin-, nor burnt-, nor any other offering, but standing by itself, (in this first part of cleansing which restores the leper to the camp,) as if representing all. It is a complementary thought, if I may so say, which while not entering into the idea of sacrifice as such, and therefore not found in these distinctive aspects of Christ's blessed work, must yet have its place in order to any just conception of what has been done.

The bird, then, represents the Lord as a heavenly Being, acquiring capacity to suffer and die in that manhood which He had taken, and which is symbolized by the earthen vessel; the living water here as ever type of that Eternal Spirit through whom He offered Himself without spot to God. It is striking that the figure does not, as we might at first imagine it would, represent the breaking

---
*In our common version, most generally given as "the fowl of the *air*."

of the *vessel*, while the bird itself escapes unhurt, but on the contrary the death of the bird itself; and Scripture is always and divinely perfect: such apparent slips are not in fact blemishes, not even the necessary failure of all possible figures, but things that call for the deepest and most reverential observation.

For it is *one* blessed Person, in whom Godhead and manhood unite forever, who has been among us, learned obedience in the path which He has marked out for us through the world, suffered the due of our sins, and gone out from us by the gate of death, risen and returned to the Father. We lose ourselves easily in this depth of glory and abasement, where the abasement too is glory; but no Christian can give up the blessed truth because of his ignorance of explanation. In ourselves we have such inexplicable mysteries, not on that account doubted, as where every nerve-pang that thrills the body is felt really not by the body, but by its (as reason would say) *untouched* spiritual inhabitant. Here it is not needful to explain, to accept the lesson: He who came upon earth to do the Father's will has taken as the means of His doing it that "prepared body" which was the instrument by which *He* accomplished it. Thus, rightly, according to the figure, the bird of heaven it is that dies in the earthen vessel. This stooping is the unparalleled marvel and power of the weakness in which He was crucified. We must not take the glory that was His to deny or lessen that weakness, but accept it as adding to it the wonder of such humiliation. How beautifully is this preserved in that one hundred and second psalm, in which, if any where, we have just this type!

"Hear My prayer, O Lord, and let My cry come unto Thee. . . . For My days are consumed as a smoke. . . . I have eaten ashes like bread, and mingled My drink with weeping; because of Thine indignation and wrath, for Thou hast lifted Me up and cast Me down. My days are like a shadow that declineth. . . . He weakened My strength in the way; He shortened My days: I said, 'O My God, take Me not away in the midst of My days; Thy years are throughout all generations!'"

Who then is this that speaks? who is this who suffers under the wrath of God, and that to death; whose days cut off contrast so with the divine eternity? How does this psalm proceed? and what is the astonishing answer to this lowly prayer?

"Of old hast Thou laid the foundations of the earth, and the heavens are the work of Thy hands. *They* shall perish, but Thou shalt endure: yea, all of them shall wax old like a garment; as a vesture Thou shalt change them, and they shall be changed: but Thou art the same, and Thy years shall have no end!"

If He go down into death, then, He must needs show Himself master of it. Resurrection must vindicate Him as the Lord of all: "Destroy this temple, and in three days I will raise it up." Accordingly in the type before us it is of resurrection that the second bird speaks. Let loose into the open field, he carries back to the heavens to which he belongs the blood which is the witness of accomplished redemption. The second bird represents the unextinguished, unextinguishable life of the first which has come through death, taking it captive, and making it subservient to the purposes of divine goodness, which, by the blood shed in atonement, cleanses us from the defilement of spiritual leprosy.

Here, for the first time, in connection with the legal sacrifices, we have the type of resurrection as necessary to the application to us of the great Sacrifice itself. "He was delivered for our offenses, and was raised again for our justification." (Rom. iv. 25.) In Isaac, long since indeed, we saw one received back in a figure from the dead, but there the results were personal to himself: there was no application of blood, no announcement of justification by resurrection. These are important features, which this type of the birds for the first time adds to the picture of atonement.

And thus it is throughout Heaven's ministry of love: not so much the Son of Man necessarily lifted up as on the other hand, so far as such types could reach, that God has given His only begotten Son. It is divine love that has been at charges to bring such ready and effectual help to human outcasts. It is to the degraded and polluted leper that the purity of heaven descends. How precious this contrast! In truth man's case was hopeless to any other than divine resources. If "it is God that justifieth," who but He could righteously justify those expressly designated as "ungodly"?

This justification of ungodly ones who are content to trust themselves as such in the hands of Christ has been once for all pronounced in the raising from the dead of Him who for our sins went into death. Abraham needed a special word in his day from God, and that availed for himself alone. For the rest, the apostle distinguishes between the "*passing over*" of sins that had been before" the cross, and the *justification* at the present time of him that believeth in Jesus.* Under this *public* justification by resurrection, announcing the acceptance of that which *actually* justifies,— the blood of the cross,—*we* come individually as soon as we believe, and need no individual declaration.

---
*See the Revised Version of Romans iii. 25, 26.

## Chapter XIII.

### *The Day of Atonement.*

THE day of atonement was that upon which the efficacy of every sacrifice in Israel depended. On that day alone was the holiest entered and the blood of atonement put upon the mercy-seat before God "once a year." This alone sanctified for them the tabernacle and all its appointments, with the altar itself.

It is of the day of atonement that the epistle to the Hebrews mainly treats, interpreting and applying its lessons for our use, though not without a side-reference to Israel themselves, when in a future day they shall find in Christ the meaning of all their shadows. It will be of profit, before we begin to consider it in detail, to see the nature of this double application, or its dispensational character, as the apostle and the book of Leviticus together present it to us.

In the twenty-third chapter of this book it finds its place among Israel's holy seasons,—not feasts, for feast it is not, but a day in which they were to rest, not in joy but in sorrow of spirit, afflicting their souls. In the order of these, the passover, first-fruits, and Pentecost (or feast of weeks) begin the year; then there is a long pause till the seventh month, and in this the rest are found: on the first day the blowing of trumpets, on the tenth the day of atonement, and on the fifteenth begins the feast of tabernacles. These seasons fall therefore into two divisions, of which the first has special reference to the Church, the second to Israel. This last begins with the blowing of trumpets, which, as the gathering of the congregation, speaks of the reassembling of Israel; then the day of atonement speaks of their repentance and taking refuge under the work of Christ; while the feast of tabernacles is the anticipation of their millennial blessing. Upon all that does not concern our present purpose we of course do not enter here, but it is evident thus that the primary reference of the day of atonement is to the last days and Israel's apprehension of the work of Christ when "they shall look upon Him whom they have pierced, and shall mourn for Him as one mourneth for his only son," and "in that day there shall be a fountain opened to the house of David and to the inhabitants of Jerusalem for sin and for uncleanness."

This gives its full meaning to the fact that in the day of atonement it is after the high-priest has come out of the sanctuary that he confesses the sins of the people on the head of the scape-goat and sends it away by the hand of a fit person into the wilderness. This is the application to the people of the work of Christ long before accomplished, and the apostle, in the epistle to the Hebrews, teaches us our part to be in connection with His going *into* the sanctuary, not His coming out. For us, *the Holy Ghost* is come out, to give us the knowledge of what is done in our behalf, adding for us two things which in the type before us find no expression: the first, the session of our High-Priest at the right hand of God; the second, that for us the vail is rent, and by faith we enter into the sanctuary itself.

The day of atonement thus, while having peculiar significance in relation to the people of Israel in a future day, covers nevertheless the whole present period; and we are led to ask, Is this application made by the apostle to us as Christians to be found in the Old-Testament type itself? And to this we are able to answer undoubtedly in the affirmative. The first offering,—for the priestly house,—is entirely distinct from that for the people; and it is Peter, the apostle of the circumcision, who teaches us to recognize our representatives in these (1 Pet. ii. 5). We shall find how much the apprehension of this distinction tends to make clear the doctrine of atonement itself.

The failure of the people had caused the forfeiture of the place conditionally promised them as "a kingdom of priests," and given Aaron and his sons their special priesthood. The failure of the priests themselves had now shut them also out of the inner sanctuary. But all this only served to bring out the condition of man as man, and his need of the Mediator of whom on this occasion Aaron was but the type. He could only in fact draw nigh thus once a year, not in his garments of glory and beauty, but in simple linen garments, and with sacrifices for himself and all the people.

Typically, these linen vestments have a glory of their own not excelled by any other. They represent the personal righteousness which, tested as it was by the fiery trial of the cross, and the unbending requirements of divine holiness, alone insured the acceptance of His work and His deliverance out of the awful place which He took for men. Crying "unto Him who was able to save Him *out of* death," He "was heard for His piety."

(Heb. v. 7, *Gr.*) It was God's "*Holy* One" who "could not see corruption." And this perfection of His it was by which as High-Priest of our profession He entered the sanctuary.

But in this respect therefore He was the total opposite of the Jewish high-priest, who, as one taken from among men, and so, like others, himself compassed with infirmity, by reason hereof comes with the blood of others in atonement for his own sins. He, on the other hand, "holy, harmless, undefiled," enters the heavens with His own blood as atonement for the sins of His people. The type in Aaron is necessarily thus deficient because *but* a type. It must of necessity bear witness to its own deficiency, and thus point forward to Him who should yet fulfill it. The deficiency itself is thus not an imperfection merely; it is rather a perfection: not meaningless, but full of meaning. And it is important to see this.

Before, however, Aaron carries in the blood of the sacrifice into the most holy place, there must be another witness to the preciousness of Christ personally. "He shall take a censer full of burning coals of fire from off the altar before Jehovah, and his hands full of sweet incense beaten small, and bring it within the vail, and he shall put the incense upon the fire before Jehovah, that a cloud of the incense may cover the mercy-seat that is upon the testimony, that he die not."

The witness of the high-priest's garment is here confirmed. If *that* might seem in question because of his personal need of cleansing by blood, *here* was an unmistakable witness. It is not sacrifice; it must not be confounded with it. It is the proclamation of the value of Christ Himself before there is the testimony to the value of His work with God. Here the fire of God's holiness tests all,— how has it tested Him!—only to bring out the fragrance of "sweet incense." This covers the mercy-seat, that in safety and in peace the priest may sprinkle it with the blood of atonement.

The sacrifices are two, as we have seen; one for the priestly house, the other for the people. Both are sin-offerings; for, as we have seen, and as Hebrews xiii. explicitly declares, only the blood of those beasts burnt outside the camp could be brought into the sanctuary. Here we find however a remarkable difference in the animals offered, the more remarkable when we contrast it with the regulations of Leviticus iv. *There*, for the congregation, as well as for the high-priest, the offering was the bullock. Here, for the high-priest it is still that, but the offering for the people is the evidently much lower one of the *goat:* and this will be found in the most beautiful way to confirm the interpretation already given of that chapter. There it will be remembered that we took the high-priest and congregation as figuring Christ and the Church. It is thus that the blood for the congregation is brought into the holy place to anoint the incense-altar: it is a *priestly congregation* that is thus figured; and this the Church is.\* But the goat is for the ruler and the common person,

---

\* The distinction in this respect cannot be maintained if in chapter xvi. 18 the "altar" is the golden altar of incense, for in this case the blood of the goat for Israel would also be put upon it; but this is not so, and the expression "before Jehovah" is inadequate to prove it. How often, and even in this chapter, is this connected with "at the door of meeting" (as ver. 7). On the other hand verse 17 shows the work completed for the sanctuary, and then Aaron "goes out" to the altar, which in 20, 33, is named apart from the sanctuary and tent of meeting altogether. It seems to me that the blood on and before the mercy-seat accomplishes all the rest.

which we have seen to give Israel's standing; and here the blood anoints only the altar of burnt-offering, not entering the tabernacle at all.

Now how striking it is to find that on the day of atonement the bullock is for the priestly house,—the Church,—while the goat is again for Israel. If we look deeper, we shall see how suitable this is. The bullock speaks of service; the goat, *merely of the place of sin being taken.* In the case of the last, if sin be removed, that is all; but the bullock speaks of service to God, the *glorifying Him* in the place thus taken; and "if God be glorified in Him, He will also glorify Him in Himself:" this opens the sanctuary to His people; He is not only their Substitute upon the cross, but their Representative in glory.

Thus in the millennium Israel, though accepted, will have place on the earth, not in heaven; and so, though in greater nearness in the new earth, while the Church has hers with her Lord according to His promise† (Jno. xiv. 3).

The bullock is first slain, and its blood brought into the sanctuary, and sprinkled once upon the mercy-seat and seven times before it. Once is enough for God; the sevenfold sprinkling is the witness of perfect acceptance before the throne. The goat being then killed, its blood is then carried in and sprinkled after exactly the same manner. And so, it is said, "he shall make atonement for the holy place because of the uncleanness of the children of Israel, and because of their transgressions in all their sins; and so shall he do for the tent of meeting that remaineth among them in the

---

† Of course it is not meant to confine this to the Church.

midst of their uncleanness." "And he shall make atonement for himself, and for his household, and for all the congregation of Israel."

Then follows the reconciliation of the altar, and then the ordinance of the scape-goat. We must look at this, and get the general features of the whole thus before us, before we look at the doctrine of atonement as expressed in it.

For the priesthood, there is but one sin-offering, —the bullock; for the people, there are two goats which together form but *one* sin-offering. Lots are cast upon the two goats; one, the Lord's lot, becomes the sacrifice; the other, when the work of atonement within the sanctuary is finished, has the sins of the people confessed and put upon its head, and bears them away to the wilderness—to an uninhabited land. It is plainly the actual removal of the people's sins, and manifestly refers to the yet future history of the people as we have already seen it, when "they shall look upon Him whom they have pierced," at His second coming, and be cleansed from their sins. We have to look at these things to see what light they give us as to propitiation and substitution, or the Godward and manward sides of atonement for sin. In general, the Lord's lot is said to illustrate propitiation; the scape-goat, substitution; but we must inquire how far this is true, and their connection with each other.

Propitiation I have called the Godward side of atonement, using the latter word in the larger sense in which we generally use it now; but in our common English Bibles no distinction of the kind appears. Atonement in the Old Testament, we may rather say, is the equivalent of propitiation in the New, which replaces it.* It has been urged that we never find God as the object of propitiation, but only "sins," and that thus the thought is rather "expiation" than propitiation. It is thus only more completely the counterpart of the Hebrew *caphar*, of which the same thing is equally true.

Yet it is also true that the Greek word used in the New Testament (ἰλάσκομαι) is one which, in its common use in that language, undeniably has the force of appeasing, and is even used once in the gospel of Luke in the passive form in this way,— our Lord putting these words in the mouth of the publican, standing afar off and smiting on his breast, and saying, "God, be merciful"—(ἰλάσθητι) "be appeased," "propitiated"—"to me a sinner" (Luke xiii. 13). As put into the mouth of such an one, its force doctrinally must not be urged too much; and elsewhere the fact is as stated above. We surely, however, cannot avoid (nor would we) the meaning of propitiation as thus introduced into the thought of expiation itself. Divine love indeed never needed to be forgotten in the heart of God toward us; it was there from eternity, and the cross, where God gave His only begotten Son, is the expression of it; but it is the expression also of demands of righteousness which required satisfaction in order to its showing forth: and this is what we mean by propitiation; it is the propitiation of otherwise withstanding righteousness, which now is turned to be on our side fully as God's love is.

---

* "Atonement" and "reconciliation" in Romans v. 11 and Hebrews ii. 17 ought, as is well known, to exchange places; and this is the only place in the New Testament in which the former word occurs. In the passage in Hebrews the word used is elsewhere translated "propitiation."

Propitiation is thus really the divine side of atonement; and he who accepts truly the one can make no difficulty as to the other: the expiation *is* the propitiation. Now let us look at this as exemplified in "the Lord's lot," "Jehovah's lot," on the day of atonement.

First, let us realize what "*Jehovah's* lot" implies. It is not "*God's* lot" simply, although Jehovah is of course God, but God in relation to His people, God in the title by which He redeems them, as the third of Exodus fully assures us. The goat which is Jehovah's lot is the sacrifice by which He maintains in righteousness this relationship, as we see by what is stated. It is thus His dwelling-place and all the means of approach to Him alone can remain among them. But this involves of necessity atonement for the sins of the people among whom He thus abides, and so it is distinctly stated: "And he shall make an atonement for the holy sanctuary, and he shall make an atonement for the tent of meeting, and for the altar, and he shall make an atonement for the priests, and for all the people of the congregation."

The goat which is the Lord's lot, moreover, as explicitly speaks of substitution as it does of propitiation. The *goat* (the type of the sinner,) is the very thing which does speak of that: no figure could more precisely convey the thought. Propitiation it proclaims to be *by* substitution, and for the people therefore for whom the substitution is, *and for no other*. Let us mark these things, for they are of great importance, if we would see clearly the relation between these thoughts. If substitution is for a certain people, then propitiation is for that same people only; if propitiation has a universal aspect, then substitution must have the same.

On the other hand, the scape-goat does not represent atonement, but only its effects. The true rendering of ver. 10 should be, "To make atonement *for* it, to let it go for a scape-goat into the wilderness." The common version, with most others, reads in exactly the opposite way,—"to make atonement *with* it," which is what is certainly not done. It is the goat that is Jehovah's lot that makes atonement for the other, and this shows conclusively what "Jehovah's lot" implies. The living goat is in this way identified with it, so that it is said, "Two kids of the goats for a sin-offering;" but its blood is not shed, its life is not given up, and this the next chapter of Leviticus shows to be absolutely necessary: "it is the blood that maketh atonement for the soul. To find any aspect of atonement itself we must look to the first goat alone.

Propitiation, then, is inferred here, and not in fact presented; and substitution is brought out clearly *in its effects*, as removing sin; while in the Lord's lot substitution is presented however none the less; as where, if not in the sin-offering, may we expect to find it? In fact, for Israel when the Lord comes, they will need the special application to them of an offering long before offered, when the day of grace might seem entirely passed.

For the priests, who represent the Church, *there is no scape-goat*. Substitution for them is found simply and entirely in the bullock of the sin-offering. It must, of course, be found there in what exactly answers to Jehovah's lot among the goats; and the apostle, in Heb. x., applies the principle of the scape-goat to Christians in the Lord's words by Jeremiah (the words of the new covenant): "Their sins and iniquities will I remember no more." And this is as far as the effects of substitution (as seen in the scape-goat) seem to reach. This, then, cannot avail to separate substitution from being essentially implied in the "Lord's lot," —in the propitiatory offering.

Propitiation, I repeat, then, is by substitution, and in no other way, and for the people alone for whom the substitution is. This may seem, to many, to narrow its application in an unscriptural way, or to widen that of substitution in a way just as unscriptural. In reality, it does neither; while it clears up many obscurities, and meets some tendencies to serious error. But let us examine Scripture.

Propitiation is evidently for no select number merely. It is for "the whole world," as 1 John ii. 2 explicitly teaches. "And He is the propitiation for our sins; and not for ours only, but also for the sins of the whole world." Here "the sins of" are in italics in our common version, showing that in the Greek there are no words exactly representing them: it is contended therefore by some that they should be omitted, and that this preserves an important difference; while the propitiation is for the *sins* of Christians,—so removing them,—it is only for the world,—their sins not being removed. And some have a similar objection, while owning that Christ died for all men, to saying that He died for the *sins* of all.

Now, assuredly, it is not true that the sins of all men are removed by the death of the Lord; and if that were meant by saying that He died for them, the use of such language in Scripture (for it *is* used) would involve the deepest perplexity. Some moreover have rashly put forth this as the gospel, that Christ has borne the sins of all, and that now men are called to believe this for themselves, being condemned only for their *un*belief of it.

But this is utterly false, for in the day of judgment we are assured that men shall be judged "according to their works," not merely for their unbelief; and Scripture no where says that Christ has borne the sins of all men. Faith can say in believers, "The Lord hath laid on Him the iniquity of us all;" but it is true of believers only.

Yet propitiation is for the sins of the whole world, and the passage in 1 John ii. is conclusive as to this. The words which are sought to be omitted are necessarily implied; for what else does "not for *ours* only" do but imply them? Had it said, "not for *us* only," it would have been entirely different; but "not for *ours* only" necessarily infers, then for the sins of others also.

Moreover, when the apostle is reminding the Corinthians of the gospel which he had preached to them, he says it was "that Christ died for *our sins*, according to the Scriptures" (1 Cor. xv. 3). But he could not preach as gospel that Christ died for other people's sins: "ours" is there plainly general, as in the epistle of John it is distinctive.

But if propitiation has this general aspect, and propitiation be by substitution, can substitution be general also? and if so, in what way? For this we must look deeper, for even the word in question is not in Scripture, although the thought is, and we cannot therefore have a simple text to appeal to, as in the other case we have.

What then is meant by substitution? It is One taking the place of others, so that they for whom He stands shall be delivered from all that in which He stands for them. The cross is thus the complete taking of death and judgment for those whom there He represents, so that for them salvation is absolutely insured. This is the substitution which the sacrifices speak of to us, and we have again and again considered it. A substitution in death and judgment can mean nothing less than the necessary salvation of those for whom it is made.

It is clear, then, we cannot speak of the world in this connection. A substitute for the world the Lord could not be, or universalism would be the simple necessity, and there could be no judgment for a single soul. But this is terrible error, and not the truth in any wise; and error which is now deceiving thousands. What have we on the other hand? "Substitution," is the thought of many, "for the *elect*." This is, of course, limited atonement. It is not possible to make it unite really with propitiation in any real sense for the world. You may say it is *sufficient* for the whole world. In itself it may be of value enough, but available it is not. Could one coming upon this warrant plead the value of that which in its design was absolutely for a limited number, of which he was not one,—Christ being really the Representative of so many millions and no others? If you say they will not come, it may be very true they will not; but you cannot say the work is done for all, if it be not so; and the blood of propitiation is the blood of substitution—of an offering offered for so many.

Another consequence follows. This offering has been offered, accepted, and Christ's resurrection is the justification of all for whom He died. Our sins were on Him, and were put away—when? Eighteen hundred years ago! But how then could *we* ever have been accounted sinners? How is justification by *faith* possible,—that is, justification *when we believe?*

These are not imaginary difficulties or results; they are actual and operative. And they are the effect—as so much error is—of misplaced truth. Election is a truth of Scripture; but election is not, in Scripture, brought in to limit the provision made in atonement,—a provision really made and sufficient for all the world. On the other hand, Christ is not a substitute for the world, for substitution implies the actual bearing and bearing away of the sins of those who are represented in the Substitute, and the sins of the world are not so borne away. He is the Substitute of *His people*, but a people not numerically limited to just so many, but embracing all who respond to the invitations of His grace, though it were indeed the world for multitude.

Thus even in Israel, though the offering of the day of atonement was for the people of Israel alone, even here the door of circumcision was kept ever open, by which the stranger might take his place at the redemption-feast, and be as "one born in the land." And circumcision was, as we know, "the seal of righteousness by faith." How precious this open door of divine grace, through all the darkness of the legal economy! Thus we have an intimation of how the *actual* Substitute for the sins of His people may be (in language suggested by another) the *available* Substitute for the sins of all. Only as come in among the number of

His people can we say, "The Lord hath laid upon Him the iniquity of us all;" for if justification be by the resurrection of the Substitute, as it truly is, it is none the less by *faith* we are justified; only as believing does it become our own.

With this the doctrine of the last Adam is in fullest accord, as the fifth of Romans represents it. For the principle is that of representation, the one for the many, and the connection between the one and the many a *life*-connection; yet is there in the last Adam's work an aspect toward all: "Therefore, as by the one offense toward all men to condemnation, even so by one righteousness toward all men unto justification of life." The family position and blessedness are open to all that will; but on the other hand, "as by the one man's disobedience the many were made sinners, so by the obedience of the one shall the many be made righteous."

Propitiation is, then, by substitution, and only so; yet the substitution itself is not for a fixed number before-determined, but for a people to whom men can be freely invited to join themselves, because of the infinite value of the work accomplished, and of the infinite grace which that work expresses. "For God so loved the *world*, that He gave His only begotten Son, that whosoever believeth on Him should not perish, but have eternal life."

## Chapter XIV.

### *The Red Heifer.* (*Num. xix.*)

THE book of Numbers gives us the history of the wilderness, the testing of the people by the trials and difficulties to which they are exposed, their failure as so tested, and the triumphant grace of Him whose love and whose resources for His people cannot fail, and whose word is pledged to bring them through. The ordinance of the red heifer gives us the effects of atonement, not in forgiveness, but in the purification of the people from uncleanness, and this in a special form, which had its peculiar significance in relation to the wilderness.

For the wilderness is, of course, the world as the place of our pilgrimage,—a place where every thing about us echoes the divine voice, "Arise ye, and depart; for this is not your rest: because it is polluted." The seal of its condition in this respect is death, in which the life universally forfeited is removed and man given up wholly to the corruption, which has already been inwardly his state.

Death marks the world as a wilderness before God, and for him therefore who has the mind of God; it is a scene of death out of which we have escaped as dead with Christ, and partakers of eternal life in Him beyond it, and separation from which is an absolute necessity to real holiness. "Pure religion and undefiled before God and the Father is this: To visit the fatherless and widows in their affliction, and *to keep one's self unspotted from the world.*" (Jas. i. 27.)

The remedy for defilement is here typically put before us. It is not in a new sacrifice, nor in the shedding of that blood without which is no remission. It is in the application of that which speaks of a sacrifice once for all completed, of wrath exhausted and gone, the *ashes* alone remaining to testify of the complete consumption of the victim. In this way the red heifer, in opposition to the many sacrifices constantly being offered, represents alone among legal ordinances the abiding efficacy of that which has been offered "once for all."

The victim is here a female,—a type of which I have already spoken. It is passivity, subjection, willessness, which we may see in the Lord in Gethsemane, whose "cup" was in fact drunk afterward upon the cross; a *red* heifer, as the ram-skins of the tabernacle were dyed red, to show how far this willess obedience in Him went. "Without spot or blemish:"—with neither defect nor deformity; and "upon which never came yoke,"—not simply sin's, but any, for a yoke is an instrument to *enforce* subjection, which in Him could not be. At the same time when He was saying, "Not My will, but Thine, be done," He might have had twelve legions of angels and gone to the Father, but would not: His was the perfection of a willess will.

And how suited all this to express the perfection of the obedience unto death, by which our disobedience was met and removed, and which is to be fruitful *in* us as well as for us, in separating us from the lawlessness and lusts which characterize us as fallen creatures!

The heifer is brought forth without the camp and slain, like any sin-offering, even the blood being burned, except what is used in the sevenfold sprinkling before the tent of meeting, where the people went to meet with God. And into the midst of the burning of the heifer were cast cedar-wood and hyssop—types of all nature, from the highest to the lowest (1 Kings iv. 33), and scarlet—of the glory of the world: "if any man be in Christ, it is new creation," and by the cross is severed his connection with the old.

A man that was clean then gathered up the ashes of the heifer, and they were laid up in a clean place outside the camp, to be kept for the congregation of the children of Israel, for a water of separation, a purification for sin.

A person defiled with the dead remained unclean for seven days; on the third day and on the seventh he was to be sprinkled with it,—running water being put to it in a vessel,—and on the seventh day at even he should be clean. The sprinkling on the third day was all-important: "if he purify not himself the third day, then the seventh day he shall not be clean."

The reference to death as the stamp upon the old creation makes all this clear. The third day is the resurrection day, deliverance from death; the eighth,—first day of the new week,—speaks of new creation. One cleansed by the evening of the seventh day was brought in fact to the eighth: only by deliverance from the old creation could he be really clean; but into this resurrection,—the resurrection of Christ,—is the necessary introduction: therefore the insisting upon the third day.

Only in the power of resurrection could death become a means of purification for the soul. We cannot be in any true sense dead to the world except in the power of a life which is ours beyond it. But thus *resurrection* is not the revival of the old, but that which links us with the new creation. This is the united teaching of this third and seventh-day sprinklings. The power of the Holy Ghost (the running, or "living," water) applies to the soul the death of the cross, that death in which for us the old world ended under judgment, to set us free from all the seductive power of things through which we pass,—free for the enjoyment of what is ours outside it. The world is but the place of the empty cross, and He who once filled it is now entered for us into the Father's house, our Forerunner. This is purification of heart for him who realizes it; power for true self-judgment, and deliverance from the corruption that is in the world through lust.

This is "water-washing by the word." The sacrifice is not again offered, nor the blood afresh sprinkled for him who is thus to be cleansed. Neither acceptance nor relationship are here in question, although just as "without holiness, no man shall see the Lord," so "he that purifieth not himself shall be cut off from Israel."

The lesson as far as atonement is concerned seems just this dependence of purification on it. The water as well as the blood comes out of the side of a dead Christ, with whom we too are dead. How shall we that are dead live any longer in that to which we are dead?

We have now completed the types of atonement; before our glance at the Old-Testament doctrine is complete, we have still to consider the prophets and the psalms.

## Chapter XV.

*Prophetic Testimony. (Isa. vi. and lii. 13–liii.)*

THE testimony of the prophetic books, distinctively so called, is full and constant to the person and glory of Christ: the announcement of His sufferings and atoning work on the other hand infrequent, and of the latter scarcely to be found, except in one passage of one book,—the fifty-third of Isaiah. Here, indeed, it is full and explicit; but we must not expect the wondrous reality to break often through its vail of type and figure while that dispensation of shadows lasted. The sacrificial system, at which we have been looking, was of course all through in existence; and Isaiah it is who is prepared for his mission, as peculiarly, and even by his very name,* the prophet of salvation, by what is in effect a sacrificial anointing. This is indeed remarkable in its character, and as the prophetic seal upon the Mosaic testimony.

"In the year that king Uzziah died I saw also the Lord sitting upon a throne, high and lifted up, and His train filled the temple. Above it stood the seraphim: each one had six wings; with twain he covered his face, and with twain he covered his feet, and with twain he did fly. And one cried unto another, and said, 'Holy, holy, holy, is the Lord of Hosts; the whole earth is full of His glory.' And the posts of the door moved at the

---
* *Jeshaia,* the "salvation of Jehovah."

voice of him that spake, and the house was filled with smoke." The holiness of God was necessary wrath in a fallen world; and in such a presence, what is man, whoever he be? "Then said I, 'Woe is me! for I am undone; because I am a man of unclean lips, and I dwell among a people of unclean lips; for mine eyes have seen the King, the Lord of Hosts.'" But if this be the necessary confession, how blessed the grace which is, in equal necessity, the divine response! "Then flew one of the seraphim unto me, having a live coal in his hand, which he had taken with the tongs from off the altar; and he laid it upon my mouth, and said, 'Lo, this hath touched thy lips; and thine iniquity is taken away, and thy sin is cleansed.'"

This touching of the "lips with sacred fire," how often has it been the subject of an allusion which has missed the whole point of what is here. It is quite true that it is a prophet whose lips are touched, and that his call (whether to the prophetic office itself or to some special mission) follows directly after; but the touch is nevertheless not that of inspiration, and the fire does not energize here, but "cleanse." And striking it is to find such an instrument employed in such a way. The live coal would seem more the symbol of divine wrath against, than of mercy for a sinner; nay, it does undoubtedly speak of that very character in God which the seraphim had celebrated, and which made His presence so insupportable to a guilty conscience. How could *such* a God give sentence in favor of one confessedly a sinner? It is easy enough *out of* His presence to imagine this,—easy enough to say that mercy becomes Him as well as righteousness; certainly, if He be (as He must be) merciful, no one was ever afraid of His loving mercy. But He must be righteous in His mercy: righteousness must guarantee and condition all its acts; nay, justification (if this be possible,) must be the act of righteousness, and of righteousness alone. And this it is that produces terror at the thought of His presence.

How blessed is it, then, to see in this live coal, the very figure of that implacable righteousness in God which must be, here actually that which, applied to a man's sin-stained lips, cleanses and not consumes them! "Lo, *this* hath touched thy lips; and thine iniquity is taken away, and thy sin is purged." But why? and how? The answer is most easy and most precious. It is a coal *from off the altar* which the seraph applies. It is a coal which has been consuming the sacrifice for sin: the type of a holiness which, while it remains of necessity ever the same, has found its complete satisfaction in that which has put away sin for every sinner convicted and confessed. Righteousness, because it is that, can only for such proclaim that "thine iniquity is taken away, thy sin is purged."

This indeed opens the prophet's lips to speak for God: "Also I heard the voice of the Lord, saying, 'Whom shall I send? and who will go for Us?' Then said I, 'Here am I; send me.'" It is no wonder that he who in this (as the apostle tells us) "saw [Christ's] glory, and spake of Him" should be the instrument to declare His blessed work with a clearness which is no where else to be found outside of the New Testament. This we must look at now, although for our purpose it will be only a few statements that we shall consider.

The prophecy begins with ver. 13 of chap. lii and goes down to the end of the fifty-third chapter. All the typical vail is dropped, and we see One manifestly in a sacrificial place for men,—a sin-bearer. The details of the death by which He would be cut off from among men are minutely given, as well as the perfection of character and life which fitted Him for an offering. He is, moreover, Jehovah's servant in all this, fulfilling His gracious purposes of blessing, and exalted by Him to glory unequaled as His sorrow.

Let us take this first, which to Him was first. It is as Jehovah's servant that the prophecy begins with Him. The wisdom with which He acts, the glory resulting, hinge upon this. God is glorified in Him; and being glorified in Him, glorifies Him in Himself. In the depths of that terrible agony to which He stooped, in the heights of supreme glory to which He is lifted, He is still and ever the steadfast servant of Jehovah's will. It pleased Jehovah to bruise Him: Jehovah hath laid on Him the iniquity of us all; Jehovah's purpose prospers in His hand; He is "Jehovah's arm" of power for the deliverance and blessing of His people. How indeed like a track of light through the darkness of this apostate world is such a course! This is the bullock of the burnt-sacrifice, offered indeed for us, but "without spot, to God."

In the world despised and rejected, that was the necessary effect of what was His true glory. In His humiliation, carnal eyes discerned but weakness; to God, He was the "tender plant" of perfect dependent manhood; but therefore not formed by circumstances—not growing out of them, as far as they were concerned with His resources in

Himself, a root out of a dry ground, life conquering death, but in strangership necessarily unknown and misconceived by those who, not being Wisdom's children, justified her not.

Yet not apart from men, to whose wants and sorrows, in no mere patronage, but as one bearing them in His own soul, He ministered; a death of shame and agony, to Him the necessary price of relieving even the least of the consequences of sin,—that death which those unconscious of their need took but as the decisive token of His own rejection.

In fact it was but the antitype of those vicarious sacrifices which for centuries had been prophesying day by day in Israel, "He was wounded for *our* transgressions, bruised for *our* iniquities." Chastisement was it truly, still for our purification, corrective discipline *for us* whose peace it made,—"the chastisement of our peace;" for "with *His* stripes *we* are healed." "The iniquity of us all Jehovah has made to meet on Him."

Under the pressure—what? Only the full proof of absolute perfection: no violence (the sin of power), no deceit (the sin of weakness); taken away by oppression with the form of judgment, stricken for the sin of others, not even a word but in meek surrender to the full weight of woe, which transformed with agony His whole frame and features. Nor was this therefore merely bodily agony: His *soul* was made an offering for trespass, travailed with men's salvation, and was poured out unto death; He numbered with the transgressors, bearing the sin of many, making intercession for the transgressors.

Already we are following the track of the white-robed priest into the sanctuary. In truth, that entrance could not long be delayed. Even in death, the appointed grave with the wicked is changed into the rich man's tomb. Life follows—length of eternal days, and the portion of a conqueror. But it is Jehovah's purpose prospers in His hand: a seed is given Him among sprinkled nations, fruit of the travail of His soul, by His knowledge turned to righteousness.

Such, in brief, is Isaiah's vision of Christ; but the Conqueror-Sufferer here depicted is without difficulty recognized as the One of whom the prophet has before spoken in terms which are full of the deepest significance. He is the "Child born," the "Son given," whose "name is called Wonderful, Counselor, the *Mighty God*, the *Father of Eternity, the Prince of Peace*" (ch. ix. 6). Weakness and omnipotence are here united; and in Him we find the Founder of that eternal state in which the purposes of divine wisdom being fully accomplished, divine love can rest without possibility of any after-conflict. The work which we have here been contemplating is that in which the foundation of this is laid. Jehovah's wondrous Servant is Himself Jehovah; and in Him God meets man in the embrace of reconciliation and of love eternal.

This is surely the gospel of the Old Testament, but we must remember here the caution of the apostle of the circumcision as to the real intelligence of even those who wrote of such infinite glories: "Of which salvation the prophets have inquired and searched diligently, who prophesied of the grace that should come unto you; searching what, or what manner of time the Spirit of Christ which was in them did signify, when it testified beforehand the sufferings of Christ, and the glories that should follow. Unto whom it was revealed that not unto themselves but unto us they did minister the things which are now reported unto you by them that have preached the gospel unto you with the Holy Ghost sent down from heaven. Which things the angels desire to look into." 1 Pet. i. 10–12.)

## Chapter XVI.

### *The Testimony of the Psalms.*

IN the Psalms we have some of the most wonderful unfoldings of the cross in its inner meaning that Scripture furnishes. It is striking that whereas in the gospel narratives themselves it is mostly the external sufferings of the Lord which occupy us, in the Psalms the divine Sufferer utters freely His heart out. The one cry of abandonment which does indeed expose its mystery, and which Matthew and Mark record, finds its full interpretation only in that twenty-second psalm, the language of which it borrows, and to which it thus guides our thoughts. And here we find, under a vail, if we may so say, the vail removed. As the priests, able to enter within the tabernacle, could behold the glories of it, so we whom faith brings within, can listen to the very heart of Christ outpoured, and see earth's failed foundations laid afresh and for eternity by One standing where no other could stand but He. Typically given, according to the Old-Testament character, unbelief may doubt or deny the revelation. It is to faith that God reveals Himself; Christ, dumb before His accusers, displays to His disciples His true glory.

There are five psalms which we shall briefly look at in connection with our subject, and which give us different aspects of the cross. Three of these—the twentieth, twenty-second, and fortieth are in the first book; the sixty-ninth is in the secnd; the hundred and second in the fifth book. I have elsewhere shown the way in which these five books of the Psalms identify themselves respectively with the five books of Moses. Here it will be seen how the Genesis-book,—the book, as we may say, of the divine counsels, maintains its character in the way in which it opens up to us the work of Christ: in the twentieth psalm, as victory over evil; in the twenty-second, as meeting the requirement of the divine nature as against sin; in the fortieth, of that which, like the sweet-savor offerings, shows the infinite moral perfection which delights in God, and in which He delights.

The twentieth psalm begins then, where the story of grace began in Eden, with the announcement of the cross as victory over the enemy. The way in which it is introduced is perfect as all else. The first book (psalms i.–xli.) divides into three parts; in the first of which we find, as connected with the sufferings and deliverance of His people, Christ rejected (ps. ii.) and glorified (viii.). His people are always here Israel, and in the second part (ps. ix.–xv.), their sufferings in the last-day crisis, out of which they are finally delivered, are detailed. In this second part Christ is not found. In the third (ps. xvi.–xli.), we have Him in a new character which, penetrating to the heart of the subject, explains and perfects the whole counsel of God. He is seen *amongst* the people in the lowly grace of perfect manhood, for God, for man, redeemer from misery as and because from sin. The sixteenth psalm thus shows Him in the place of dependence and trial, God His one portion and sufficiency in that path that passes through death itself into the joy of His immediate presence:

the path of life through death, for us henceforth open.

Thus the seventeenth psalm shows how He can now associate others with Himself; giving the righteous through the only righteous One their ground of appeal to God. While the eighteenth psalm speaks of His victory over all His enemies, a victory which involves others with whom He is pleased to associate Himself.

The next three psalms show, on the part of His people, the faith which attaches them to Him. In the nineteenth psalm, first of all, setting its seal to God's other testimonies of creation and the law, but to rest only with full satisfaction and delight (in the two following psalms) in Him who is alone their kinsman-redeemer. While psalm xxii. completes the picture by adding to the knowledge of redemption by power that of redemption by purchase, "not with silver and gold, but with the precious blood of Christ, as of a lamb without blemish and without spot."

The twentieth psalm is in other respects a remarkable one, but, as far as we have now to do with it, is of very simple character. The anointed (or Messiah), king of Israel, is seen in distress and difficulty in the presence of his enemies (compare xxi. 8, 11). It is conflict on account of others; and the name of the God of Jacob—*i.e.*, of grace toward sinners, is appealed to in his behalf. From the sanctuary in Israel, and out of Zion, seat of electing love, the help is to come. It is connected with the establishment and triumph of the people plainly, and Messiah's offerings and burnt sacrifice secure this. Hence, in his deliverance they rejoice aloud, and in the name of this God set up their banners. Jehovah, their covenant-God, saves, and to the king also (to Messiah Himself) they call. The next psalm enlarges upon this deliverance and victory.

The twenty-second psalm now unfolds the reality of the sacrifice upon which all is based. It is the well-known psalm of atonement, so solemn and so dear to the Christian heart. It is the sin-offering, —the requirement, as I have elsewhere said, of the divine nature. The forsaking of God is the necessary result of the holy One being made sin.

This is what is throughout put in contrast with all other sufferings. All felt as they are, and no indifference to any,—the bodily anguish, the shame, the heartless wickedness of the assailants,—yet the one agony which outweighs all the rest is this forsaking of God. "My God, My God, why hast Thou forsaken Me? far from helping Me, from the words of My roaring? O My God, I cry in the day-time, and Thou hearest not, and in the night-season, and am not silent!" "Be not far from Me, for trouble is near; for there is none to help." "But be not Thou far from Me, O Lord: O My strength, haste Thee to help Me!"

This forsaking is also carefully distinguished from any thing that a righteous man ever suffered. "Our fathers trusted in Thee; they trusted, and Thou didst deliver them: they looked unto Thee, and were delivered; they trusted in Thee, and were not confounded. But I am a worm, and no man." Yet a long line of martyrs witness to us that, as to deliverance simply from the hands of enemies, multitudes have cried and not been delivered, the sufferings through which they passed only proving that they were not forsaken, but on the contrary maintained and enabled for whatever they passed through by a power manifesting itself thus the more. How many before and since have proved Paul's experience, "Persecuted, but *not* forsaken"! None of these patient sufferers, precious and acceptable as their patience was to God, touched even the border of the darkness of the cross,—when the cry of the holy One found no response.

What to Him that desertion was, He Himself alone could know. "Thou art He that took Me out of the womb; Thou didst make me hope even upon My mother's breasts; I was cast upon Thee from the womb; Thou art My God even from My mother's belly." To us, born in sin and shapen in iniquity, to whom estrangement from God is the natural condition, and who, even when by grace redeemed, can so readily slip out of communion with God, how little is it possible to realize the agony of this condition! With us, too, when out of communion, it implies a state which prevents realization. The spiritual sense is blunted, the spiritual affections are not in play; and if even in this state sorrows and troubles surprise us which make us feel vainly after Him, the consequences of the terrible loss are sure to overshadow and obscure the spiritual loss itself; while at the most the darkness that can envelop one who has ever known God is the darkness of a clouded sun compared with a night of total absence in the case of Him who was made sin for us.

Alone in human weakness, with every element of bitterness in the dreadful cup which was His to drink,—He could ask, as none among men beside could, "*Why* hast Thou forsaken Me?" yet proclaim at the same time the holiness of Him who had forsaken Him. "But Thou art holy: dwelling amid the praises of Israel." Is not here, in fact, the reason of this forsaking, that the holy One would dwell amid the praises of a redeemed people? That worship could never be but for the cross. He must be in the outside place of darkness, that we might be, children of light, in the light with God.

The consequence is, that after He has been brought into the dust of death, and is heard from the horns of the unicorns, the blessing that flows out answers in perfect contrast to the suffering endured. The Son of God, as the fruit of His own abandonment, communicates to now-acknowledged "brethren" the Father's name. He who was in that unique, solitary place, praises in the midst of the congregation which He gathers, and whose praise He leads. Yea, "the meek shall eat and be satisfied: they that fear the Lord shall praise Him:" the heart of the redeemed shall taste the joy of eternal life (26). To the ends of the earth, and to perpetual generations, the wave of blessing spreads,—joy out of sorrow, praise out of desertion, light out of darkness, life out of death; the subjection of adoring worshipers to a Saviour-God, and His righteousness declared in the accomplishment of this great salvation.

Thus ends the wondrous twenty-second psalm, of which atonement in its central feature—He who knew no sin made sin—is the theme throughout. Any full exposition is not here within our scope. But it is the foundation of all true blessing to understand it; its words will give the deep tones to our praise forever.

A number of psalms follow which give us, in very various character, the exercises and experiences which find their answer in, or are the fruit of, this blessed work. At the close of the book are two psalms which give, by way of conclusion, as it were, the moral of the whole. The heart of Christ is shown in its innermost depths, His life in its one principle, in the fortieth psalm. In the forty-first the heart of man is seen in relation to Him who has come into the place of poverty and reproach for men—into a humiliation so low that unbelief can misconceive and discredit His true glory.

The fortieth psalm is significant in its very number, which is that of perfect probation; and here again we find the Lord in those sufferings which were the trial of His perfection, and which brought out the sweet savor of His blessed sacrifice, here put in contrast with all other sacrifices.

In the twenty-second psalm we have seen the Lord taking the sinner's place, that God might dwell among the praises of His redeemed; here we see what was in His heart Godward who did so. It is the perfect Man, with ears which never needed the anointing of blood to consecrate them to God; who, marked out in the book of God's counsels from the beginning, now comes forth simply, as none else, to do the will of God; His law within His heart. "By which will," says the apostle, "we are sanctified by the offering of the body of Jesus Christ once for all." This perfect devotedness He manifested there where, in the sharpest and most terrible contrast to it, He cries, "Mine iniquities have taken hold upon Me, so that I am not able to look up; they are more in number than the hairs of My head; therefore My heart faileth Me." Yet, says He, "I waited patiently for the Lord;" even in the "miry clay" of that "pit of destruction."

Plainly this is the psalm of burnt-offering, though the sacrifice represented take the place of all the other offerings. Indeed it is quite in character that it should be so. The burnt-offering was the "continual burnt-offering," as that which was emphatically a sweet savor to God. The sin-offering is what the necessity of man craves and obtains; so with the trespass, and so with the peace-offering; but the burnt-offering, as it goes wholly up to God, expresses that which is the object of His unceasing delight. Thus, when no other sacrifice was there at all, the burnt-offering kept its place upon the altar, which from it, indeed, received its name; for this blessed work it is in which the moral glory of His person (which is what the altar speaks of) shines out most fully.

Here, accordingly, it is not the outside place that His cry expresses, but the "iniquities" which, as taking them upon Him, He could call "Mine:" this was the miry clay of the pit into which He who came to do God's will had descended. This, therefore, is the character of suffering most suited to display, as a dark background, that personal glory. Unbelief might indeed take such confession to justify its rejection of the holy One, while faith, adoring, finds in it its eternal blessing. And this is the key to the psalm which follows this.

### *The Testimony of the Psalms.—Continued.*

THE next psalm of atonement we find in the last section of the second book. And here, whatever difficulty of interpretation may attach to it otherwise, there is nothing to dim the assurance that the sixty-ninth psalm gives us the trespass-offering. The very word for sins—"My sins are not hid from Thee"—should be rather "trespasses." While the restitution character of the trespass-offering comes out with unmistakable plainness in the fourth verse,—"Then I restored that which I took not away." In the words of the eleventh verse we may discern with little more difficulty the ram of the trespass-offering. The difficulties of the psalm belong rather to its exposition, which I am not attempting here. With this brief notice, therefore, we may pass on to the final psalm.

This is the hundred and second, whose place in connection with the book to which it belongs is full of interest. The fourth book speaks, as the fourth book of Moses does, of the world as the scene of man's strangership through sin. Its first psalm, the ninetieth, shows him thus; his link with eternal blessedness snapped with his link with God. It is a strain of the wilderness, a lament over that generation of men who because of their unbelief died there, and who thus could be used as a fit exemplification of the general condition. The Lord, man's dwelling-place, has been forgotten. He who brought man from the dust bids him return to it. Sin and God's righteous anger explain this terrible anomaly. "Thou hast set our iniquities before Thee, our secret sins in the light of Thy countenance; for all our days are passed away in Thy wrath; we spend our years as a tale that is told." The psalm concludes with a prayer: "Return, O Lord, how long? and let it repent Thee concerning Thy servants;" but no ground is given for such repentance till we come to the following psalm.

And here we have, not the first man, but the second; and in plain contrast to the first. Man has forgotten the name of his God: how clearly this comes out in Moses' question at the bush!— "And Moses said unto God, 'Behold, when I come unto the children of Israel, and shall say unto them, The God of your fathers hath sent me unto you; and they shall say unto me, What is His name? what shall I say?'" (Ex. iii. 3.)

But this lost name of God is the key to man's condition. It reveals him as a wanderer (how far!) from the Father's house, "without God in the world; without, therefore, a hiding-place from the forces of nature now in league for his destruction! How wonderful that "a *Man* shall be as a hiding-place from the wind, and a covert from the tempest,"—a Man, but the "Second Man"! It is He who, abiding in the secret place of the Most High, shall lodge under the shadow of the Almighty; He who in the path of faith takes Jehovah for His refuge and fortress, His God, in whom He trusts. Here is One who, at least for Himself, can claim fully the divine protection—an unfailing, perfect Man.

But how does this avail for *men ?* God's name revealed is "Jehovah;" and "Jehovah" is "the God of redemption"—the name under which He intervened to redeem His people of old. Redemption, too, by power is seen in the following psalms. Jehovah's throne is established upon earth; the wicked are destroyed; the righteous flourish. The earth also is set upon a permanent ground of blessing—"The world also is established, that it cannot be moved." Jehovah comes (xcvi.–c.) to His restored creation; which claps its hands, rejoicing in His presence.

This closes the first half of the book, but the fullness of the blessing is not yet told out, nor the ground of it. This, redemption not by power but by purchase, and at the hands of the Kinsman-Redeemer, can alone disclose.

In the hundred and first psalm we find accordingly once more the Second Man, into whose hands now the earth is put, King of Israel evidently, but with another name and a wider title soon to be declared. For in the hundred and second psalm, not only Zion's time of blessing is come, but for the earth also to be blessed, "when the peoples are gathered together, and the kings also, to serve the Lord."

But all this blessing waits upon One who in the meanwhile is seen, not only in human weakness, but under the wrath of God. Alone in the presence of His enemies, His heart smitten and withered like grass; and why? "Because of Thine indignation and wrath; for Thou hast lifted Me up and cast Me down."

But how then is the blessing to come, if Israel's King, the Second Man, upon whom all depends, is cut off under the wrath of God? "He weakened My strength in the way; He shortened My days. I said, 'O My God, take Me not away in the midst of My days: Thy years are throughout all generations.'"

What, then, is the answer to this prayer? It is the amazing declaration as to this humbled One:—

"Of old hast *Thou* laid the foundations of the earth; and the heavens are the work of *Thy* hands: they shall perish, but Thou shalt endure; yea, all of them shall wax old like a garment; as a vesture shalt Thou change them, and they shall be changed: but Thou art the same, and Thy years shall have no end."

Thus Creator and Redeemer are the same wondrous Person: Jehovah, whose throne is set up upon earth, is that very Second Man into whose hands the restored earth is given; and this, and the blessings resulting from it, the hundred and third and hundred and fourth psalms celebrate. This weakness of man is the power and grace of God for man's salvation. God's name is indeed decisively declared, and man finds his happy hiding-place in God Himself, never to be a wanderer again.

How fit a conclusion to the picture of atonement which the Psalms, and indeed the whole of the Old Testament, present! May our joyful adoration grow in equal pace with our apprehension of them.

CHAPTER XVII.

*Atonement in the New Testament. The Gospels.*

WE now come to the New Testament. We have already carried its doctrine with us in the interpretation of the Old; for our object has been, not to trace the gradual unfolding of the truth from age to age, but to get as completely as possible for our souls that truth, as Scripture, now complete, as a whole presents it to us. Thus we have already anticipated much of what would otherwise now come before us. Yet we shall find, if the Lord only open our eyes to it, abundance of what is of unfailing interest for us, and that the substance here goes beyond all the shadows of the past.

In the Gospels, however, the doctrine of atonement is but little developed. We have instead the unspeakably precious work which wrought it. The Acts also, while devoted to the history of the effects of its accomplishment, speaks little directly of the atonement itself. It is not till we come to Paul's writings that we find this fully entered into, and its results for us declared. He is the one raised up to give us the full gospel message, as well as the truth of the Church, of both of which he is in a special sense the "minister" (Col. i. 23, 25).

The gospel of John, however, more than all the rest together, does dwell upon the meaning of the cross; and here it is mostly the Lord Himself who declares it to us. John's is, in a fuller sense than the others, the Christian gospel; and in it, we may say, we enter into that holiest of which they see but the vail rent at the end; while for John, the glory typified by that of the tabernacle of old shines out all through.* It is necessary, then, to show how this is possible, man at the same time being fully shown out for what he is by the light in which he stands. Before we speak of this, we must take up, however, the "synoptic" gospels, and briefly examine their testimony.

Their direct teaching is scanty indeed. The Lord's own declaration that "the Son of Man . . . . . came to give His life a ransom for many," and that His blood was "shed for many," is given in all; Luke indeed changing this last into "shed for *you*," and Matthew adding, "for the remission of sins." The doctrine of atonement is quite plain here, however little enlarged on. Luke gives us beside how, after His resurrection, He appears to the two on the way to Emmaus, and reproves them for their unbelief of all that the prophets had spoken, adding, "'Ought not Christ to have suffered these things, and to enter into His glory?' And beginning at Moses and all the prophets, He expounded unto them in all the Scriptures the things concerning Himself." Afterward, to the eleven He says, "Thus it is written, and thus it behoved Christ to suffer and to rise from the dead the third day, and that repentance and remission of sins should be preached in His name, beginning at Jerusalem."

When we look more deeply at the work pre-

---

* John i. 14, where "dwelt" should be, as in the margin of the Revised Version, "tabernacled:" it is a plain reference to the glory of old.

sented in these three gospels, we find in them respectively, as I have elsewhere shown, the features of the trespass, sin, and peace-offerings respectively. The trespass-offering unites with Matthew's gospel of the kingdom as being the governmental aspect of atonement—the reparation for *injury* rather than judgment for *sin;* yet this in its Godward side reaches of necessity to the vindication of the holiness of His *nature*, so that Matthew and Mark alike give the forsaking of God. But while the three gospels show the rending of the vail, and the holiest opened, Matthew alone shows the meeting of death for us, the graves giving up their dead; for death is governmental infliction, and so belongs to Matthew's theme. So, evidently, does that view of the cross which is found in the two parables of the kingdom, the treasure and the pearl, where the work is looked at as a governmental exchange—a purchase: "went and sold all that He had and bought it."

Mark, while it has the forsaking of God also,— the characteristic features of the sin-offering,— omits these governmental features. It is the Son of God in the glory of His voluntary humiliation, obedient even unto death, glorifying God at His own personal cost,—as the bullock is the highest grade of the sin-offering,—but therefore glorified of God in consequence, so that He ascends to the right hand of God (xvi. 19). But His humiliation is most absolute. He does not, as in Matthew, "dismiss His spirit" (xxvii. 50, *Gr.*), as One that had power to retain it, but, in true sin-offering character, "expires" (chap. xv. 37, *Gr.*). Even in His cry upon the cross there is a note of difference which is significant. He says, not "Eli,"—literally, although it be a name of God, "My *Strength*,"—but "Eloi," "My *God*."\*

So the results of the cross are characteristically different in Mark from Matthew. It is not a commission given to disciple into the kingdom, but to preach the gospel, with power over the enemy and over the consequences of sin accompanying the simple believing in this precious word.

In Luke, the peace-offering character is everywhere plain, as it is in the cross most manifestly. It needs scarcely comment. The Lord's cry is "Father;" and He openly assures a dying thief of a place with Him in paradise. But further exposition would belong rather to a sketch of the gospels than of the doctrine of atonement, and it has been given elsewhere.

The gospel of John introduces a subject in the Old Testament unrevealed,—eternal life. Personally, the Lord was this, and among men the light of men. But this only disclosed the truth of their condition. The world—and the Jews in this light were only part of the world,—lay in a darkness which no light merely could reach, for it was the darkness of death; but a spiritual death of sin which not even life alone could reach. Guilt must also be met. "Except a corn of wheat fall into the ground and die, it abideth alone," are our Lord's words. Life must spring for man out of an atoning death. The water of cleansing and the blood of expiation must come out of the side of a dead Christ. The Spirit thus bears record that "God has given to us eternal life."

The first word as to atonement in the gospel of

---

\*In the twenty-second psalm it is "Eli," not "Eloi," but I think it clear that the latter, in this connection, is the deeper word.

John is in the Baptist's testimony: "Behold the Lamb of God, who taketh away the sin of the world." This is the broad general view of Christ's work and its effect. By and by, a "new" earth—not *another* earth, but the earth made new as to its condition,—will be eternally the abode of righteousness (2 Pet. iii. 13). To us, how wonderful a condition for this world, which for nearly six thousand years has been the abode of sin, to be the abode of everlasting righteousness! What will have accomplished this? The precious sacrifice of the Lamb of God. Every inhabitant of that new earth will be one redeemed by the blood of Christ, and secured eternally by its value. Sin will be completely banished. Its memory only will remain, to give full melody to the praises of the saints.

But who is this Lamb of God? "This is He," says the Baptist, "of whom I said, 'After me cometh a Man which is preferred before me, for He was before me.'" After in time as a man, yet the One inhabiting eternity! It is God Himself who is at the cost of redemption, and that when not power merely could redeem, but only blood! Therefore a man, incarnate, to be in meek surrender of Himself a Lamb slain. This is what is of moral value to fill the earth with righteousness, and to lift to heaven also those made members of Christ by the baptism of the Holy Ghost (i. 33).

In the next case, the need of man has just been fully exposed in the Lord's words to Nicodemus. He must be born again, as Ezekiel had already witnessed; although not able to declare the full truth and magnitude of this work of God in man. But One was come from heaven to declare it, Son of Man on earth, yet still in heaven. Nor only to declare it, but to make this work possible; for "as Moses lifted up the serpent in the wilderness, so also must the Son of Man be lifted up, that whosoever believeth in Him should not perish, but have eternal life."

The imperative necessity of atonement is here affirmed. The Son of Man *must* be lifted up, and faith in Him be the way of everlasting life. The type of the brazen serpent shows in what character "lifted up;" for Moses' serpent clearly represented that by which the people in the wilderness were perishing. At bottom, for them as for men in general this was sin, the poison of the old serpent, which has corrupted the nature of every one born of flesh. For this, "made sin," Christ was "lifted up,"—offered to God a sacrifice,—that men might have, by faith in Him thus offered, not a restoration of mere natural life, but one spiritual and eternal.

But again we are assured of who it is effects the sacrifice. Not only it must be One who as Son of Man *could* be lifted up, but "God so loved the world, that He gave His only begotten Son, that whosoever believeth in Him should not perish, but have everlasting life." It is not only the Son of Man, lifted up to God, but the Son of God in the full reality of this, the *eternal* Son, the *only* begotten, sent down, God's gift, from God.

Thus eternal life is ours who believe. The character, privileges, and accompaniments of which are detailed for us in the chapters that follow. The sixth chapter shows it to us as a life enjoyed in dependence, lived by faith, maintained by the meat given by the Son of Man—*meat* which endures to everlasting life, as long as the life itself does. But this meat is the bread from heaven, and the bread is His flesh, which He gives for the life of the world. But this involves His death,—bloodshedding; so that "except ye have eaten the flesh of the Son of Man, and *drank His blood*, ye have no life in you; he that eateth My flesh and drinketh My blood hath eternal life,—abideth in Me and I in him. As the living Father hath sent Me, and I live because of the Father, so he that eateth Me, he also shall live because of Me." (*vv.* 53, 54, 56, 57.)

We must notice a difference here which neither the revised nor the common version makes apparent. The first expression—"*have* eaten," "*have* drunk,"—speaks of *once* partaking, the others of continuous. The once having eaten and drunk insures eternal life, but it is maintained as a practical life of faith by continuous eating and drinking. It is a life dependent though eternal, and what communicates it sustains it also.

The tenth chapter presents the Lord as the Shepherd of the sheep, giving His life for them, in perfect freedom, and yet as fulfilling the commandment of the Father. He is thus able to give a reason for the Father's love (*v.* 17), and they are saved, have eternal life, and can never perish, nor any pluck them out of His hand. In the twelfth chapter, again, He compares His death to that of a corn of wheat which dies to produce fruit; but I pass on to consider the character of the closing chapters.

Here, what is a feature every where, is just this voluntariness of self-surrender which the tenth chapter has declared. No one takes His life from Him: the men sent to take Him fall to the ground before Him, and while giving Himself up, secures the safety of His followers by an authoritative word. To Pilate, He declares His kingdom founded on the truth, and which every true soul would recognize; while the authority of the governor over Him existed but by divine permission for a special purpose. Upon the cross, there is no darkness and no weakness. He declares His thirst, to fulfill one final scripture, then announces the perfect accomplishment of His work, and delivers up His own spirit to the Father. The soldiers' errand doubly fulfills the prescient word of God, who on the one hand guards the body of His holy One from mutilation, while on the other giving to man the threefold witness of completed atonement. All this speaks of the offering for acceptance (Lev. i. 3, 4, *Rev. Vers.*), the voluntary burnt-offering.

To this the account of the resurrection answers also perfectly. Relationship established, the corn of wheat having died to bring forth fruit, the Lord owns His "brethren," ascending to His and (thus) their Father, His and their God. He assures them of peace, the fruit of His work (xx. 19, 20); of their new-creation place in connection with Himself, last Adam (*v.* 21; comp. Gen. ii. 7, 1 Cor. xv. 45), and of their qualification therefore to "receive the Holy Ghost." All this is the testimony of perfect acceptance in the value of His completed work.

The Acts, while speaking throughout of the *fruits* of atonement, give little of the doctrine of the work itself. We may therefore pass it over. I am aware of no new aspect in which it is presented to us in it.

## Chapter XVIII.

### *Romans and Galatians.*

THERE are four of the epistles of Paul which introduce us by successive steps to the height of Christian position. They are those to the Romans, Galatians, Colossians, and Ephesians. As our position before God is in the value of Christ's work for Him, we shall necessarily find in these epistles the exposition fully of the doctrine of atonement. In fact, a concordance is enough to show that only in Corinthians and Hebrews beside, of Paul's fourteen epistles, is the *blood* of Christ spoken of, and only in Philippians additionally is the cross. Hebrews, indeed, speaks more of the blood of Christ than any other book of the New Testament. Its doctrine we shall hope to consider at another time, however.

Of the four epistles I have mentioned, Romans and Galatians are most nearly connected together, and Colossians and Ephesians. The negative side of deliverance by the death of Christ is the topic of the former; the positive side of what we are brought into as identified with Him in life, that of the latter; although Colossians unites the "dead" and "buried with Christ" of Romans to the "quickened" and "raised up with Christ" of Ephesians.

Romans and Galatians differ mainly in this, that while Romans through the ministry of Christ's work establishes the soul in peace, and delivers it from the power of sin, Galatians takes up the moral principles of Judaism and Christianity as a warning to those made free by grace, not to entangle themselves again with the yoke of bondage. In pursuance of this end, Galatians takes one important step beyond Romans, although clearly involved in the doctrine of the latter. Romans says we are dead with Christ to sin and the law; Galatians adds that we are crucified to the *world*, and a *new creation*.

The doctrinal part of Romans is found in the first eleven chapters: the part with which we have to do here is the first eight, and these divide into two portions at the end of chap. v. 11. Up to this, we have the doctrine of the *blood* of Christ as justifying us from our *sins*. Beyond it, we have the doctrine of the *death* of Christ as meeting the question of our *nature*.

Yet the blood is the token of death, and as this alone, has meaning. The difference is mainly in this, that the blood is looked at here as what is *offered to God;* the death, as what *applies to us*. It is, in fact, the death of our Substitute which is offered to God in the blood of propitiation. We look Godward to see the effect for us as to peace; we look at the sacrifice to realize the power and fullness of what has satisfied Him. The two are bound together in the most indissoluble way. To him for whom the blood of Christ avails, the death of Christ at the same time applies; while the order of apprehension is undoubtedly that in which the epistle treats of these. The first question with the soul is, Is all settled forever Godward? The next is, If this be so, *how* is the evil *in* me looked at by God? Much else connects itself with this, but our theme here is the atonement, and to this I confine myself at this time.

In accordance with what has just been stated, we find in chap. iii. 23 Christ first of all spoken of as a "propitiatory," or "mercy-seat,"* "through faith in His blood." Access to God is the point, with ability to stand before Him. "All have sinned, and come short of the glory of God"—the glory that abode upon the mercy-seat, but from which all in Israel were shut out. This language of the old types is as simple as it is profound in its significance for us. The ark with its mercy-seat was the throne of Him who dwelt between the cherubim, of whom it was said, "Justice and judgment are the foundation of Thy throne," but at the same time "mercy and truth go before Thy face." (Ps. lxxxix. 14.) How then could the reconciliation of these toward man be accomplished? Only by the precious blood typified by that toward which the faces of the cherubim looked, the value of which the rent vail has witnessed, and through which the "righteousness of God" is now "toward all," the sanctuary of His presence is become the place of refuge for the sinner. By the sentence of His righteousness we are justified according to His grace, a sentence publicly given in the resurrection of Jesus our Lord from the dead, "who was delivered for our offenses, and raised again for our justification."

"Much more, then, being now justified by His blood, we shall be saved from wrath through Him. For if when we were enemies we were reconciled to God by the death of His Son, much more, being reconciled, we shall be saved by His life." This is of course His life as risen for us, as He

---

*$iγαστήριον$, the regular word for "mercy-seat" in the Septuagint; not $iγασμός$, "propitiation," as 1 Jno. ii. 2.

says Himself, "Because I live, ye shall live also."

This leads on to the second part of Romans, where our death with Him and our life in Him are dwelt upon. And as the first part has given us the blood of the sin-offering,—blood which alone could enter the sanctuary,—so the second gives us the burning of the victim upon the ground, the passing away in judgment of all that we were as sinners before God. "God sending His own Son in the likeness of sinful flesh, and for sin, condemned sin in the flesh." Thus we have a new place and standing in Christ wholly, the old relationship to sin and law being done away.

Propitiation and substitution characterize thus these two parts of Romans respectively. The connection shows us clearly what we have before looked at, that it is *by* substitution that propitiation is effected. The propitiation is indeed marked as for all, though of course effectual only for those who believe. The door is open for all into the shelter provided, but he who enters finds in the substitution of Another in his place the only possible shelter. Upon all this it does not need now to dwell, as this has been done elsewhere, and we may now pass on to look briefly at the epistle to the Galatians.

Galatians, as to the doctrine of atonement, adds but little to Romans. The apostle, opposing the introduction of the law among Christians, insists strongly upon his own authority as one raised up of God, in His grace, out of the midst of Judaism, the incarnation of Jewish zeal against the Church, called to be an apostle of the revelation of Christ which he had independently received. He was an apostle, neither from men nor through man, and had got nothing even from other apostles who were such before him, and who had been constrained to recognize the grace that had been given to him. Peter, moreover, at Antioch, had been openly rebuked by him for giving way to the legal spirit which he was now opposing; and here he repeats the doctrine of Romans which he had then maintained, that not only we are "justified by faith in Christ and not by the works of the law," but also that "I through the law am dead to the law, that I might live unto God; I am crucified with Christ."

Afterward, he goes on to show more particularly the purpose of the law, and, as illustrating this, the manner in which God had given it, with its character as shown by all this. The promise to Abraham had been made four hundred and thirty years before the law, in which God had declared that the blessing for all nations should be through his Seed—Christ, and on the principle of faith. But law is not faith; its principle is that of works, righteousness through these, but therefore for man only curse for every one who was upon that principle; and that the blessing of Abraham might come upon the Gentiles God had to remove this curse of the law out of the way, Christ taking it when hanging upon the tree, for the law had said, "Cursed is every one that hangeth upon a tree."

Two things need a brief notice here. First, that (as should be obvious, but to some is not,) the hanging upon the tree is not *itself* the curse, but only marks the one upon whom the curse falls. The curse itself is no external thing, but a deep reality in the soul of him that bears it. This was the wrath upon sin which Christ bare for us, the forsaking of God, which, had it not been borne, assuredly no blessing could have been for any.

Secondly, therefore, *it was not for Jews alone*, or those under law, that the curse of the law was borne. The words of the apostle are surely plain here: "Christ hath redeemed us from the curse of the law, being made a curse for us, . . . *that the blessing of Abraham might come upon the Gentiles through Jesus Christ;* that we might receive the promise of the Spirit through faith." Clearly he says that blessing could not have been for Gentiles had Christ not borne the curse of the law, and this is as simple as possible, as soon as we see what essentially the curse is.

It is not the question whether Gentiles were under the law. It is quite true that God never put them there; and the apostle, in the passage before us, distinguishes those redeemed from its curse from the Gentiles of whom he speaks. But the law was only the trial of *man* as man, and Israel's condemnation by it was, "that *every* mouth might be stopped, and *all the world* become guilty before God." (Rom. iii. 19.) It is to miss fatally the point of the law not to see in it this universal reference. "As in water face answereth to face, so the heart of man to man." The condemnation of the Jew is the condemnation of all: the law's curse, only the emphasizing of the doom of all. And had not this been met and set aside, the blessed message of grace could have no more reached the Gentile than the Jew himself.

This is the very purpose of the law, for which it was "added" to the promise before given, not as a condition for it to be saddled with, but to bring out the need of the grace which the promise implies. "It was added *for the sake of* transgression" (*v.* 19, *Gr.*); not to hinder but to *produce* it, ("for where no law is there is no transgression,") to turn sin into the positive breach of law, and thus to bring out its character, and bring men under condemnation for it. But it was added also for a certain time,—"*till* the Seed should come to whom the promise was made."

But if God were thus testing man, it was by "elements of the world" (chap. iv. 3), necessarily bondagē only to the believer, and the cross is that by which we are "crucified to the world" (chap. vi. 14). For "in Christ Jesus, neither is circumcision any thing, nor uncircumcision, but a new creation" (*v.* 15). And Christ "died for our sins, that He might deliver us out of this present evil world, according to the will of God and our Father." (chap. i. 4).

It is evident that Galatians takes up and completes the doctrine of Romans by adding that of deliverance out of the *world* to that from sin and law, as well as our place in new creation, involved already in the truth of the first Adam being the figure of Him that was to come, in whom we are.

## Chapter XIX.

### *Colossians, Ephesians, 2 Corinthians.*

THE epistle to the Colossians has for its keynote the ninth and tenth verses of the second chapter—"In Him dwelleth all the fullness of the Godhead bodily. And ye are complete in Him." It is the fullness of Christ for the Christian. The first chapter gives us the first part of this, which it anticipates: "For all the fullness was pleased to dwell in Him." The second and third chapters show our completeness in Him: His death for us delivering us from our natural portion; His resurrection bringing us into our portion now with God.

In the first chapter, the work of atonement is represented as for the reconciliation of heaven and earth, as well as having accomplished the reconciliation of all believers: "And having made peace through the blood of His cross, by Him to reconcile all things unto Himself,—by Him, I say, whether they be things on earth or things in heaven. And you, that were some time alienated and enemies in your mind by wicked works, yet now hath He reconciled in the body of His flesh through death, to present you holy and unblamable and unreprovable in His sight."

This doctrine of reconciliation is important as showing how far the need and value of the cross extend. In Romans already there is the statement that "when we were enemies, we were reconciled to God by the death of His Son;" but here it extends much more widely, and has to do, not merely with persons even, but with things—all things, both in heaven and in earth. There are no persons in heaven to be brought back by the work of Christ, "for verily He taketh not hold of angels, but of the seed of Abraham He taketh hold" (Heb. ii. 16, *Gr.*). It is not, therefore, of persons that the apostle is speaking here, but of the frame-work of things put out of joint, as it were, through sin, as far as sin has reached, and which the work of Christ was needed to set right.

In this application of reconciliation two things are plain: first, that it is not merely a moral effect on man that is intended by it, (although this moral effect there is, and it is a great truth too;) and secondly, that it was in the nature of God Himself that the deepest need of atonement lay. Going on to Ephesians, we find the apostle speaking of "the redemption of the purchased possession" (i. 14); and in Hebrews ix. 12, saying, "It was necessary, therefore, that the patterns of things in the heavens should be purified with these, but the heavenly things themselves with better sacrifices than these." Here, the heavenly things, then, are spoken of as purchased, purified, reconciled, redeemed. In whose eyes were they, then, impure? Clearly, in His to whom alone all true sacrifice was ever offered. It was the nature of God which required atonement, His holiness that needed satisfaction in it. In a deeper sense than probably Eliphaz knew could it be said, "The heavens are not clean in His sight" (Job xv. 15). The work of Christ enables Him to lay hold upon all that with which sin has been connected, and restore to more than all its pristine beauty and excellency. How unspeakable is the value of that work which not only does this, but actually glorifies Him in filling the heavenly places with those redeemed from the fall, and made the very "righteousness of God in Christ."

As for Christians, they are already reconciled through the work of Christ: "You . . . hath He reconciled." It is done, although not yet are all the fruits reaped of this. Already are we before God in Christ, "accepted in the Beloved," waiting for the adoption, the redemption of the body, to put us in our place every way, in the very image of the heavenly. Reconciliation on our part necessarily includes the change from enmity, the natural state, to love, as here and in Romans both: "When we were enemies, we were reconciled to God by the death of His Son;" "You, that were sometime alienated and enemies in your minds by wicked works, yet now hath He reconciled." The moral effect is what is needed as to us. The power of the display of the love which has so wonderfully met our whole necessity brings our hearts back to God. Love wins love: "we love Him because He first loved us." Hence, for this effect, the freeness and fullness of the gospel are essential. "'Tell Me, therefore, which of them will love him most?' 'I suppose that he to whom he forgave most.' 'Thou hast rightly judged.'" Question of the love that calls forth my love is fatal to this effect. I must be delivered from the necessity of seeking my own things, in order to live, not unto myself, but unto Him who died for me and rose again. This, the apostle tells us, was the secret of his life, such as we know it was: "The life which I live in the flesh

I live by the faith of the Son of God, who loved me, and gave Himself for me."

Reconciliation was needed thus on our part, and in order that it might be, the death of Christ must meet the demand of divine righteousness; but on this very account it is never said in Scripture, as it is so often in human creeds, that *God* is reconciled by the work of Christ. He had not changed, but we. God had never enmity to the work of His hands, however fallen away from Him. He had not, then, to be reconciled; and so, even where the reconciliation is of things, not persons, it is still these that are said to be reconciled, as we have seen. As to man, reconciliation is pressed upon him on the ground of Christ's work: "We pray, in Christ's stead, be ye reconciled to God; for He hath made Him to be sin for us, who knew no sin, that we might be made the righteousness of God in Him."

The second part of Colossians gives, as I have said, the effect of the work of Christ for us, bringing in His resurrection and life beyond death as giving us our new place in the efficacy of it with God. We have "dead with Christ," "buried with Christ," almost exactly as in the second part of Romans, our death being called here "the circumcision of Christ," or Christian circumcision. While the "alive in Christ" of Romans is here carried back to its commencement in our being "quickened together with Christ." Our life in Him is thus seen, from its first moment, to be the result of atonement. The blotting out of legal ordinances, which were contrary to us, and the spoiling of principalities and powers, are connected also with His work. Risen with Him, we are in spirit to be outside the scene we are passing through,—to "seek those things which are above, where Christ sitteth at the right hand of God."

Ephesians, as is well known, carries us one step beyond this. We are not only risen, but ascended, "made to sit together in heavenly places in Christ Jesus." Here, "with" can no longer be said, as is evident. We are not actually, but as yet only represented, there: it is "the exceeding greatness of His power to usward who believe, according to the working of His mighty power, which He wrought in Christ when He raised Him from the dead, and set Him at His own right hand in the heavenly places."

This is individual, of course. And though, as in Colossians, "we have redemption through His blood, the forgiveness of sins, according to the riches of His grace," yet the meeting our responsibility in grace is not the special subject of Ephesians, but the new creation which we are made in Christ, and this in its heavenly character the epistle sets before us. It is not within our scope just now to enter upon this. In connection with it, the effect of the cross is spoken of as breaking down the middle wall of partition between both Jew and Gentile, both man and God. This middle wall of partition is the law, which the apostle calls, therefore, by a strong figure, the "enmity," and its abolition, our peace and reconciliation: "Having abolished in His flesh the enmity, the law of commandments contained in ordinances; for to make in Himself of twain one new man, making peace; and that He might reconcile both unto God in one body by the cross, having slain the enmity thereby." There is nothing here but what is simple enough, and needs no comment. Nor does Ephesians present us with any further development of the doctrine of atonement.

The texts we have had before us naturally connect themselves with one already quoted in connection with them, but to which we must give now more particular attention. It is 2 Corinthians v. 21. The whole passage runs thus: "And all things are of God, who hath reconciled us to Himself by Jesus Christ, and hath given to us the ministry of reconciliation; to wit, that God was in Christ, reconciling the world unto Himself, not imputing their trespasses unto them; and hath committed unto us the word of reconciliation. Now then we are ambassadors for Christ, as though God did beseech by us, we pray in Christ's stead, be ye reconciled to God. For He hath made Him to be sin for us, who knew no sin, that we might be made the righteousness of God in Him."

Notice, first, there is no statement here of the world having been reconciled. It is of the attitude which God took in Christ come into the world, of which the apostle is speaking. What Christ was doing when here, he says, we are doing as His representatives, "in His stead," now He is no longer here. But that attitude is of beseeching men *to be* reconciled,—not telling them they are. In this way God was not imputing their trespasses to them, inviting them to draw nigh to Him, not forbidding access.

*Now* this same liberty of access is proclaimed, but the ground of it is an already accomplished work: "He hath made Him to be sin for us, who knew no sin." The main feature of atonement is here very clearly given; and the force is made plainer by the contrast of words and thought. In the same sense was Christ made sin for us as that in which we are made righteousness; and as the sin was the sin of man, so the righteousness is the righteousness of God. Moreover, as it was not in Himself that He was made sin, for He knew none; so not in ourselves are we made divine righteousness, but in Him. The antithesis in all this no one can doubt to be designed; and it makes evident the meaning of the whole. Christ who knew no sin was identified with it upon the cross; we as the fruit of His work, in our place in Him, are identified with the righteousness of God. In Him dying upon the tree is seen the sin of man; but the righteousness of God is seen, wonderful to say, in sinners being accepted in the Beloved.

But you may say, Is not the righteousness of God seen also in the cross? Surely it is; and so the third of Romans states: "Whom God hath set forth to be a propitiation through faith in His blood, to declare His righteousness;" but in what respect? "That He might be righteous, justifying"—pronouncing righteous—"him which believeth in Jesus." That we might be in Him, it was necessary that He should be made sin for us; the righteousness of God no less could satisfy. That we are in Him declares therefore the cross God's method of salvation—affirms that righteousness, now our shelter and defense, "the righteousness of God over all them that believe." With this, then, we are identified forever: forever we shall display it, as we shall "the exceeding riches of His grace."

## Chapter XX.

### *Hebrews.*

THE epistle to the Hebrews gives, as the epistle to the Galatians does, the contrast between Judaism and Christianity, but in a different way. Galatians is written to Gentiles, to deliver them from the law as a "yoke of bondage" to which they were being subjected by Jewish teachers; it dwells, therefore, upon the character of the law as the elements of the world, a world to which as Christians we are crucified,—upon its curse, from which Christ's work had to deliver: upon the moral, therefore, not ceremonial part. Hebrews, on the other hand, is written to the Jews themselves, though of course believing ones, and takes up the ceremonial part, that in which faith ever found its refuge when oppressed with the sense of guilt, to show that here also Judaism necessarily failed, witnessing, as it was designed to witness, to that which was the substance of its shadows, now come, and by which its place was irrevocably taken. Among these typical ceremonies, those which had to do with cleansing have in this way a special place; and thus the question of sacrifices—above all, of Israel's great day of atonement—comes to be a prominent topic in the epistle.

There are thus two apparently contradictory aspects of these legal types, but which are in fact in perfect accord with one another: on the one hand, their typical likeness to the things they represent; on the other, their entire unlikeness as to real efficacy. "The law, having a shadow of good things to come," was "not the perfect image."

This appears in the very beginning of the epistle, in which the day of atonement is evidently in view, when it is said of Christ that "when He had by Himself purged our sins, He sat down at the right hand of the Majesty in the heavens." The Jewish high-priest put indeed the blood of atonement upon the mercy-seat once a year; but so far from sitting down there, he was not again permitted to enter throughout the year. For him, as for all the people, the face of God was hid,—clear proof that he had not purged the sins of any, in truth, as before Him. Judaism means God hidden and inaccessible: Christianity, sins purged and man brought nigh.

After dwelling upon the glory of Him who could effect this, as contrasted with angels, through whose ministration the law was given, in the second chapter the apostle shows us the Son of God become Son of Man, and tasting death for every man, with the purpose of bringing many sons unto glory. He who sanctifieth and those who are sanctified are all of One, on which account He is not ashamed to call them brethren. The children which God hath given Him being "partakers of flesh and blood, He also Himself took part of the same, that through death He might destroy him that had the power of death,—that is, the devil; . . . . for on the seed of Abraham He layeth hold. Wherefore in all things it behoved Him to be made like unto His brethren, that He might be a merciful and faithful High-Priest in things pertaining to God, to make propitiation for the sins of the people."

All through, once more, the day of atonement is plainly in view, upon which this passage becomes therefore a most instructive comment. "Propitiation"—which no one doubts to be the proper word, instead of "reconciliation," in ver. 17,—is here said to be expressly for the sins of the people; and the true people of Christ are interpreted to be the "seed of Abraham," clearly embracing all and only those whom as children given to Him He is not ashamed to call His brethren. With these there is a double link of connection. The sanctified and the Sanctifier are all of one, so that He is not ashamed to call them brethren. And then, because they are partakers of flesh and blood, He Himself also takes part of the same; this is on account of propitiation needed, although, as we know, He does not take manhood temporarily, but eternally. Thus, while it is true that the Lord tasted death for every man, yet it is for His people He makes propitiation; of the seed of Abraham He taketh hold. It is the kinsman-redeemer of Leviticus xxv.

In the fifth chapter we are given to see the "holy linen coat" with which the high-priest enters the sanctuary. This always speaks of practical righteousness, and the truth correspondent to it we find in ver. 7-9: "Who in the days of His flesh, when He had offered up prayers and supplications, with strong crying and tears, unto Him that was able to save Him out of [not "from"] death, *and was heard for His piety;* though He were a Son, yet learned He obedience through the things which He suffered; and being made perfect, He became the author of eternal salvation to all them that obey Him, called of God a High-Priest after the order of Melchisedek." Thus the perfection of His obedience is that by which the Lord is delivered out of death: it is God's "Holy One" who cannot "see corruption." Raised up from the dead by the glory of the Father, He is "saluted," as the word means "as High-Priest," and enters the sanctuary. It is still the day of atonement that is before us, although with the added truth as to the order of His priesthood, which is not of Aaron, but Melchisedek.

In the ninth chapter, the apostle takes up, with unmistakable plainness, the same type: "But Christ being come, a High-Priest of good things to come, by a greater and more perfect tabernacle, not made with hands—that is to say, not of this building, neither by the blood of goats and calves, but by His own blood, entered in once into the holy place, having obtained eternal redemption; . . . . for Christ is not entered into the holy places made with hands, which are the figures of the true, but into heaven itself, now to appear in the presence of God for us; . . . Christ was once offered to bear the sins of many, and to them that look for Him shall He appear without sin"—that is, apart from it, having no more to offer for it,—"unto salvation." Our place as Christians, then, is found between the entering in of the high-priest into the sanctuary and his coming out again, when Israel's sins will be removed, as ceremonially they were by the typical scape-goat: for us, in the meanwhile, the result of our great High-Priest's entrance into the heavens is known by the Holy Ghost come down. We know that, having by Himself purged our sins, He is set down at the right hand of the Majesty in the heavens,—that He has obtained eternal redemption for us. "By one offering He hath perfected forever them that are sanctified." Thus our conscience is at rest, and we have ourselves present "boldness to enter into the holiest by the blood of Jesus, by a new and living way which He hath consecrated for us through the vail—that is to say, His flesh." Our privilege—nay, our responsibility is to "draw near with a true heart, in full assurance of faith."

Finally, the day of atonement is that to which the principle of the last chapter most fully applies, the bringing into the holy place the blood of those beasts whose bodies were burnt without the camp. The complete judgment of sin must needs be before heaven can open to the worshiper. The judgment of the world is found in this, and the setting aside of the "camp" of Judaism. The Christian position is founded upon that which is the condemnation of the world, and is therefore outside it, as it is inside the vail, as brought to God.

In all this, it is evident that Christians answer to the priestly house, as we saw when going through the type in question. For these, the bullock is provided for a sin-offering; yet in the seventeenth verse of the tenth chapter the principle of the scape-goat is applied to them: "Their sins and iniquities will I remember no more." In these various references we shall find, if we compare them, the full type of Israel's great day unfolded to us, while that is added which none of the types of Judaism could convey. Upon this I do not think it needful to dwell further at present. The epistle to the Hebrews gives us the most connected, detailed teaching as to atonement which we shall find in the New Testament, and with it we may almost close our notice of the Scripture-passages; we have then, if the Lord permit, to see how far we can put together the various features which have been presented to us of this so wondrous work. It is the theme of an eternal song, which here on earth already it is ours to sing.

## Chapter XXI.

### *The other Apostolic Writings.*

THERE are but three other books which require now some attention before we close our consideration of Scripture-texts. They are the first epistles of Peter and John, and the book of Revelation.

We must not expect to find here the full development or application of atonement which Paul had especially in his commission to make known. The truth of it is every-where insisted on, however, in due connection with the peculiar theme of each book.

The theme of Peter's epistle is the path through the world of those who, as partakers of the heavenly calling, are strangers and pilgrims in it. Addressed to the believers among the Jews of the dispersion, he brings out the contrast between their Jewish hopes and those to which they had been now begotten by the resurrection of Jesus Christ from the dead. Already they had received the salvation of their souls, being redeemed by the precious blood of Christ, and born again of the incorruptible Word, and were a spiritual house, a holy priesthood. As children of God, they were the subjects of His holy government, under the discipline of a sorrow which He made fruitful, passing through a world through which Christ had passed, adverse to His as to Him. To do well, suffer for it, and take it patiently was their lot, having Him for their example, and the glory into which He had already entered their eternal rest.

It is not strange, therefore, that it is the "*sufferings* of Christ" upon which the apostle insists; that *He* suffered for *sins*, and that we must suffer, not for these, but for righteousness or for His name's sake (ii. 19-21); that He "suffered in the flesh,"—His only connection with sin being in suffering on account of it; we must arm ourselves therefore with the same mind (iv. 1).

But the sacrificial character and efficacy of His work are fully maintained, for "Christ also once suffered for sins, the just for the unjust, to bring us to God," and "Himself bare our sins in His own body on the tree,"—the practical end of this being enforced, "that ye being dead unto sins, should live unto righteousness—by whose stripes ye were healed" (ii. 24). And thus we are "redeemed, not with corruptible things, as silver and gold," (alluding to Israel's atonement-money,) "but with the precious blood of Christ, as of a Lamb without blemish and without spot" (i. 18, 19). Salvation, and begetting to a living hope, are therefore connected with the resurrection of Christ from the dead (iii. 21; 1. 3).

This is so similar to the first part of Romans that it is scarcely necessary to enter into it more here. It gives us only a part of it however, the application being plainly to the practical walk, as that in Romans is mainly to the setting free the conscience before God.

The second epistle of Peter has but one word, which we may notice as we pass on: the false teachers, who privily bring in damnable heresies among Christians, deny the "Lord that bought them." Thus the plain difference between redemption and purchase is made clear. The Lord has title to the world and all in it (comp. Matt. xiii. 44) by the cross, but we may *buy* what we have no personal interest in. Redemption speaks of heart-interest in the object, and of release, deliverance.

The first epistle of John gives us the characters of eternal life in the believer as now manifested in the power of the Spirit which is in us as Christians. He dwells, therefore, more upon the Godward side of the work of Christ—propitiation for our sins (ii. 2; iv. 10), from which, therefore, we are cleansed by the propitiating blood (i. 7). It is thus that divine love is declared toward us; and this love is perfected with us, giving us boldness in the day of judgment, in the assurance that even now, in this world, we are as Christ is (iv. 17). This falls short of Paul's doctrine, not as to the perfection in which we stand, but only in not bringing us into the heavenly places, or that of being risen with Christ. Its application is to the entire freedom of the conscience by propitiation through a substitute, whose acceptance is therefore ours.

In the last chapter we have another beautiful testimony to the necessity and perfection of the work of Christ. He came, not by water only, but by water and *blood*. And the Spirit also bears witness, because the Spirit is truth. This, without any question, refers to the blood and water that followed the soldier's spear, and of which John by the Spirit bare record (Jno. xix. 34, 35). What, then, is the purport of the record? That out of a *dead* Christ—His work accomplished—expiation and purification flow together for us. "Except a corn of wheat fall into the ground and die, it abideth alone, but if it die, it bringeth forth much fruit." Thus, as soon as He has died,—as soon as the judgment due has been borne, purification and expiation are found for men, in Him who has borne the judgment.

But, says the apostle, "this is the record, that God has given unto us *eternal life*, and this life is in His Son." In "eternal life" he sums up, as it were, these two things. For "life" is the opposite of judgment, and implies that it is passed. (Comp. Jno. v. 24, 29, where "condemnation" and "damnation" are the same word—"judgment.") While the full extent of man's need as to purification is declared. Life in a new source alone meets it. But God's grace abounds over all man's need. This life is eternal life, and in His Son,—a *divine* spring which guarantees the perfection of what flows from it.

In the book of Revelation, finally, the name the Lord bears everywhere through it shows how central as to all God's ways is the work of atonement. The book of His counsels finds none with title to open it save One who, coming forward in the character of Judah's Lion, is seen, in that which gives Him title, as the Lamb slain. He is therefore at once the object of worship by the elders as the Author of redemption: "For Thou wast slain, and hast redeemed us to God by Thy blood out of every kindred and tongue and people and nation" (v. 6, 9).

The book of life is accordingly "the book of life of the *Lamb slain*" (xiii. 8; xxi. 27); and the being written in this book is the only possible escape from the judgment of the second death (xx. 15).

Thus the saints overcome the accuser by the

blood of the Lamb (xii. 11); their robes are washed and made white in His blood (vii. 14); and this it is that gives "right to the tree of life" and to enter in by the gates into the heavenly city (xxii. 14, *R. V.*).

The throne, moreover, is the "throne of God and of the Lamb" (xxii. 1, 3); and "the Lord God Almighty and the Lamb are the temple of" the new Jerusalem (xxi. 22); and the glory of God doth lighten it, while the Lamb is the lamp thereof (*v.* 23).

Fittingly, thus, does Scripture close its testimony to the atonement and Him who made it. We will not try to define the meaning of these glorious sayings. They shine by their own light. May our attitude be that than which a creature can know no higher: that of the elders in the presence of their Redeemer—of worshipers.

## Chapter XXII.

*What Christ Suffered in Atonement.*

WE have finished our brief review of the direct Scripture-texts. It remains to look at the doctrine as a whole which they declare.

And here, while my purpose is in no wise controversy, it is hardly possible, and I think not desirable, to forget the different views obtaining among professing Christians. They differ, in fact, widely: for as atonement is the very heart of divine truth, so it sympathizes with every part of it; and there can be no material deviation from the doctrine of Scripture without its being accompanied by a correspondingly defective or distorted view of this central one.

I do not propose to give examples now, although we shall find many, no doubt, before we reach the close of these papers. The simplest course seems to be to take up the doctrine as the Word presents it to us, and then compare it point by point, so far as may seem to be profitable, with other views.

That there was a deep necessity for atonement the Lord Himself declares: "The Son of Man *must* be lifted up." No debate as to this can be admitted therefore. It is a thing to be received by faith alone. And this necessity has its ground in the divine nature, as the truth of reconciliation, as we have seen, most strongly declares. "Things in heaven and things in earth" needed thus to be reconciled. Universalism goes wrong entirely here, in substituting *persons* for things: but the fallen angels are expressly stated to be *not* those for whom Christ's work was wrought: "He taketh not hold of angels, but of the seed of Abraham He taketh hold" (Heb. ii. 16, *marg*.). But of things in the heavens it is said, "It was *necessary* that the patterns of the things in the heavens should be purified with these, but the heavenly things themselves with better sacrifices than these" (Heb. ix. 12). It was in God's sight therefore, as Eliphaz says, the heavens were not clean, and that on account, of course, of the sin of the angels. God's nature therefore—His holiness—demanded the atonement, and thus only could even the heavens be reconciled. How much more, then, as to fallen man!

As plainly it is declared in these very scriptures by *what* alone atonement could be made. "And almost all things are by the law purged with blood, and without shedding of blood is no remission" (Heb. ix. 22). This is only the echo, somewhat emphasized, of the statement of the law itself (Lev. xvii. 11): "For the life of the flesh is in the blood; and I have given it to you upon the altar to make atonement for your souls; for it is the blood that maketh atonement for the soul."

Clearly it is death therefore—a sacrificial death —by which atonement is effected. The *shedding* of blood means, not merely death, but a violent death; and only such, and that of a designated victim, could provide the altar with what availed before God. No suffering in *life* could at all take the place of this, or be included in it: these two things are wholly different. As it was death that had come in upon man through sin, so it is death alone by which his condition is met and deliverance found for him. For those under death, death the penalty must be endured.

It is plain, then, at once that God's way of atonement is not by any mere "*substitute* for penalty," as many say, but by the endurance of the penalty itself. But this is much more manifest when we consider what is involved in death as the due of sin. For, as the mark upon a fallen creature, it is the sign of a changed relationship with God the Creator; and, if it be not the end of all, it is (except mercy interpose,) the definitive introduction to a *state* of judgment which must abide as long as that which provoked it abides.

From this we must distinguish indeed the judgment of the great white throne, when every thing is made fully manifest, and the unsaved "dead are judged according to their works" (Rev. xx. 12). This is at a time when death is ended and over, although ended for these only by a "resurrection of judgment" (Jno. v. 29, *Gk.*). But in the meanwhile, the Lord's picture of the rich man, not in "hell" yet, as our ordinary version gives it, but in *hades*, with brethren yet alive upon the earth, assures us of torment already endured there in the flame of God's wrath (Luke xvi.). To this distinction we shall have yet to return: it is sufficient to draw attention to it here.

Death, then, (for the unsaved) introduces into a fixed state of judgment: fixed because the sinful condition which calls it forth is fixed. And of this, death itself is the sign; for it is the removal of the fallen creature out of the place for which he was

## ATONEMENT.

created, as unfit to remain there. Death therefore itself preaches of a penalty beyond itself.

Was this, then, part of the penalty upon man which atonement was to meet and remove for the saved? If so, it is necessarily a much heavier part. And if God's way of atonement be not by a "substitute for penalty" but by the endurance of the actual penalty itself, then the cross must be the bearing of wrath as well as death, and this must be emphasized correspondingly in Scripture. And this is in fact the case.

At first sight, indeed, it is not apparent; nay, the appearance is all the other way. "Blood," "death," as we have seen, are insisted on; and as the one need exclusively, we might at first conclude. And the general belief of Christians has been full and clear as to Christ's dying for our sins, much vaguer or less certain as to wrath-bearing. But there is a reason for this character of Scripture-testimony. Death is, as is plain, the plain mark which God has attached to sin, and His wisdom is apparent in it. It brings the sense of judgment home to the hearts and consciences of carnal men, incapable of receiving any more spiritual appeal. God deals in it with men without faith, too blind to see the things unseen naturally, too far away to know the misery of distance. Hence the great public testimony dwells on that which all can feel. Who knows not the awful feeling of that which wrenches from our grasp, and in the most unexpected times and ways, the objects of our dearest affections, and sends us out at last from all the scene and things with which we are acquainted—out, alone, out of the world, naked as we came into it, but now conscious of our nakedness, and with our conscience preaching of the things beyond? Hence all through the law, as I have elsewhere dwelt upon,* it is death that is taken up, reasoned of, pressed home upon men. Even the text used almost universally in another sense than that intended, "The soul that sinneth, it shall die," speaks not explicitly of the second death, but of the first, but of thus dying *in one's sins* indeed, and the future under the dread shadow of this. But upon this it needs not to enter here.

The sacrifices necessarily bear a similar testimony. The death thus pressed on men as the penalty of sin is that which the atoning victim bears, and bears away its sting. This is not all, but it is what is prominent; and even when we come to the New Testament, the style of testimony remains, although it is now in speech from which all obscurity is removed. The plain facts, external and manifest to all, are most insisted on,—that "Christ died for our sins according to the Scriptures; and that He was buried, and that He rose again the third day according to the Scriptures" (1 Cor. xv. 3, 4).

Faith, with a more earnest look, discovers more. The death of the cross, was it no more than other death? That, the contemplation of which wrung the Lord's soul with agony, was it physical suffering merely, or a martyr's lot? The forsaking of God, which He deprecated yet endured, was it simply the being left in the hands of His enemies, or a deeper reality?

These questions admit but of one answer. The death of the cross had its inner significance, not in being the punishment of a slave or of a criminal,

---

* "*Facts and Theories as to a Future State,*" chap. xxiii: "The Ministry of Death."

though both of these it was, but a death of curse according to the law; and there was in this a design of God in our behalf. "Christ hath redeemed us from the curse of the law, *being made a curse* for us; for it is written, 'Cursed is every one that hangeth on a tree:' that the blessing of Abraham might come upon the Gentiles through Jesus Christ; that we might receive the promise of the Spirit through faith" (Gal. iii. 13, 14). Surely it is a great mistake which some have made, to suppose that this curse from God is exhausted in the mere fact of the hanging on a tree. This is only the outward sign of it in fact, the reality consisting in the *attitude of God* toward Him who hung there. Nor, if this *be* the reality, could it be imagined that this should have significance only for Israel, as those only under the law. In fact, the Gentiles are directly stated here to be partakers of the blessing flowing from this marvelous humiliation of our Lord. Here, nothing else than wrath-bearing can fulfill the meaning—terrible as it is—of being "made a curse."

Nor could physical suffering, nor persecution of enemies, have forced from Him the bloody sweat of Gethsemane, or been the cup He pleaded not to drink. Many a martyr, strengthened by divine grace, has drunk such a cup, if that were all.

And the forsaking of God,—the very words of the blessed Sufferer guide us to that twenty-second psalm, in which prophetically it is all explained; the depths of His heart are told out here into the anointed ear of faith, and we find indeed that which is the one exception in all God's ways with the righteous. "Our fathers trusted in Thee; they trusted, and Thou didst deliver them; they cried unto Thee, and were delivered; they trusted in Thee, and were *not* forsaken: but I am a worm, and no man!" Then all the long agony is described by One with no callousness, keenly alive and sensitive to it all; while yet from it all He turns to Him on whom from the womb He had been cast, to deprecate the one sorrow far beyond all others: "Be not far from Me!"—"But be not Thou far from Me, O Lord! Oh, my Strength! haste Thee to help Me!"

There is no question that can justly arise as to whose are these words. David certainly himself had no experiences such as these. The bones out of joint, the piercing of hands and feet, the parting of His garments and casting lots upon His vesture, and then the blessing flowing out even to the ends of the earth when finally He is heard,—all this assures us beyond the possibility of doubt as to who really speaks. If we turn to the types we see in the sin-offering, in the victim burned without the camp, and upon the ground without an altar,—figures of which we have already seen the meaning—the shadow of all this; while at the cross itself the three hours of darkness was its answering shadow. God, who is Light, had withdrawn; but the result is for us a rent vail, darkness forever removed, and God in the light for us forever.

In Hebrews, finally, we have the emphatic assurance that only the blood of those victims burnt without the camp was brought into the sanctuary—that is, fully into the presence of God—for sin; and that Jesus, therefore, that He might sanctify the people with His own blood, suffered without the gate: yet another significant token of the same solemn truth.

## ATONEMENT.

Thus the penalty upon men is fully borne. It is not a *substitute* for a penalty that is found in all this, but the actual penalty itself endured. True substitution on the Lord's part is seen, as everywhere witnessed in fact throughout the Word: the iniquity of all His people so laid upon Him that He can say, as in the fortieth psalm He does say, "*Mine* iniquities." Standing thus as representing them, a true sin-bearer, God's face is hidden from Him. As in the hundred and second psalm, which is again His voice, where He cries out, "Because of Thine indignation and wrath, because Thou hast taken Me up and cast Me down."

It is on the cross, and on the cross alone, that He bears sin, as the apostle says, "Who His own self bare our sins in His own body *on the tree*" (1 Pet. ii. 24). It has been attempted to prove that this should be rendered "carried our sins up *to* the tree," and the new version gives this as an alternative in the margin. This has been fully investigated by another,\* and I do not propose to enter upon it. Every translation that I am aware of gives at least the preference to the common version; and the doctrine of Scripture admits of no other construction. Contrast the Lord's words in the twenty-second psalm, "Thou hearest not," with those at the grave of Lazarus, "I knew that Thou hearest Me *always*" (Jno. xi. 42); or, "My God, My God, why hast Thou forsaken Me?" with those elsewhere, "And He that sent Me is with Me: *the Father hath not left Me alone;* for I do always the things that please Him" (Jno. viii. 29). Who cannot see here the infinite difference? If hearing and

---

\*"The Bearing of 1 Peter ii. 24." (J. N. Darby; now to be found in Vol. viii. of his Collected Writings.)

not hearing, forsaking and not forsaking, are but the same thing, or can consist together, then words have no longer any meaning. The cross is thus distinguished from all the Lord's sufferings beside as the place where " He was made sin for us who knew no sin," and He who "is of purer eyes than to behold iniquity, and that cannot look at sin," turned away His face from the Sin-bearer.

The distinction between "offering" and "offering up" in connection with the sacrifices is here of importance. These are different words in the original, and different thoughts. The latter is the same as the word "bare" in the passage in Peter, and it is found similarly in Heb. ix. 28: "Christ was once offered to *bear* the sins of many;" where indeed both words are found. It occurs again in Heb. vii. 27, twice: "Who needeth not daily, as those high-priests, to offer up sacrifice, first for his own sins, and then for the people's; for this He did once, when He offered up Himself." It is found again, chap. xiii. 15: "By Him let us offer the sacrifice of praise to God continually;" in Jas. ii. 22, "When he had offered Isaac his son upon the altar;" and again in 1 Pet. ii. 5, "To offer up spiritual sacrifices, acceptable to God by Jesus Christ." The second word, in much the most common use, speaks simply of "presenting," and is thus applied to "gifts" as well as "sacrifices." It is the common word for "offering" as simple presentation, while the former one is that used for offering in the fire upon the altar.

Now in the passover we find that the lamb was to be killed the fourteenth day of the month at even, having been kept up first four days, being taken on the tenth day. In these typical ordinances all was significant, the numbers as all else; and they will be found in full accordance with what we find as to the Lord. His life on earth divides into three parts also: thirty years in private, (the Lamb not taken;) between three and four years of public ministry, (the Lamb taken, but not slain;) and then the suffering of the cross. The *ten* days mark the first period as that of His own personal responsibility as man. It is for this reason we have but the very briefest notice of Him in all that time. At the close, he comes forth from His retirement to take up the work for which He had come into the world. He is baptized of John in Jordan, the river of death, to fulfill all righteousness, Himself the only One upon whom death had absolutely no claim. There the Spirit of God seals Him in testimony to His perfection as man, while the Father's voice bears public witness to Him as His beloved Son. He has thus offered Himself for the sacrifice, and the Baptist owns Him as the "Lamb of God" (Jno. i. 29, 36.)

But the "four days" are yet to run before He is offered up; and this number speaks of "proving," now not in private capacity, but in His fitness for the blessed work He has undertaken to perform. Accordingly this time begins with the temptation in the wilderness, and the whole course of it is of what He calls afterward His "temptations" (Luke xxii. 28). But all demands upon Him are only the means of displaying His glorious perfections. It is this which abides for us now in those *four* gospels which have stamped upon our hearts the image of a Saviour. But in them we find therefore, not One under the judgment of God upon sin, (how dark a cloud would that be over so bright a picture!) but One speaking the Father's words, doing the Father's works, in communion with and manifesting the Father.

Finally, in the garden He delivers Himself up, and is led as a lamb to the slaughter; on the cross iniquities are laid upon Him, and this is marked by the supernatural darkness so misinterpreted by the mass of Christians. Before and after this we hear Him saying, "Father;" in it He says but "My God." Out of it He comes to fulfill what still remains by giving up His spirit to the Father; and dying with the declaration of the complete accomplishment of His work, the blood and water, in answer to the soldier's spear, show expiation and purification to be now both provided—man's need to be fully met.

Chapter XXIII.

*The Penalty in its Inner Meaning.*

BUT we have now to look more particularly at the penalty which the Lord endured for us. Penalty we have seen it was, and true substitution; Christ dying, not upon *occasion* merely of our sins, but *bearing* them in His own body on the tree—our iniquities laid upon Him, so that He calls them "Mine." No words could express more plainly a real substitution.

We have seen too that in the penalty upon man there were two parts, separable at least, if not in fact separated: the wrath of God upon sin, and death—not the second, but what came in at the beginning through sin; and that both parts He endured.

Death has its power in this, that it is the removal of the sin-ruined creature out of the place for which he was created. "Sin has *reigned* in death," as the expression is in Romans v. 21. It is man's destruction by the judgment of God, as being already self-destroyed.

But the death he dies is not the death of Sadducean materialism, but one in which the sinner abides under the judgment to which it has consigned him. It is a condition of darkness—outer darkness—for God has finally and forever withdrawn Himself. It is torment in the flame of necessary anger against sin. These are the elements of a judgment which will not be altered in character, when in the resurrection of judgment the dead stand before the great white throne to receive the discriminate awards of the day of manifestation.

Unspeakably solemn is it to consider that the holy and beloved Son of God, Himself knowing no sin, yet as "made sin for us," entered into that awful darkness, and was tried by the fire of God's wrath against it. So indeed it was. He was the Substitute under our penalty, and endured the penalty. Ours it was of course, not His; but He endured it, and endured it as the necessity of holiness, to set His people free.

But there is a point here it is important to guard, and which, guarded, will go far to preserve us from some excesses which people have gone into with regard to substitution. We must not confound the Lord's standing in our place to take for us our dreadful due, with any calculation, essentially lowering as it is to the very righteousness which it is meant to uphold, of *so much suffering for so much sin*. In the day of final award it is indeed said that "the dead" are "judged out of the things which are written in the books, according to their works" (Rev. xx. 13), and this it is, no doubt, that has been carried back as a principle to the day of atonement. It has been argued that if our iniquities were laid upon Him,—if He bare our sins in His body, then these must all have been counted up and weighed, and He must have suffered so much for each one. In this case it is plain we have just so many sins absolutely provided for, and no others. It is a limited atonement of the most rigid kind, and of which it would be impossible to use the language of the apostle, "A propitiation, not for our sins only, but also for the sins of the whole world" (1 Jno. ii. 2). For if the sins of the whole world had been *after this manner* provided for, no one could be lost, or judged again for what in Him had received its judgment. And this is very far from the truth of Scripture.

A propitiation for the sins of the world means nothing less than such a provision made for them that if the whole world turned to God through Christ, it would find in Him a complete Saviour. But if sins needed thus to be individually taken into account and settled, this would not be true; if they *had* been thus settled, they could not in any case come up in the day of judgment; and this is what some hold—that men will be judged for nothing but for the refusal of grace in Christ: but this is entirely hopeless to prove from Scripture, which declares they shall be "judged according to their works," and that "every one shall receive the things done in his body according to that he hath done, whether it be good or bad" (2 Cor. v. 10). And, as the Preacher says, "God shall bring every work into judgment, with every secret thing, whether it be good, or whether it be evil."

"A propitiation for the sins of the whole world" does not, then, mean such an individual settlement of sins, nor is this needed in order for salvation. Can it, then, be needed for "*our* sins" any more than for the sins of the whole world? or can we make propitiation in the one case have a meaning which it has not in the other? This is surely impossible to suppose in the Word of God. Its faithfulness refuses absolutely all chameleon colors.

The sufficiency of atonement for the whole world we must absolutely receive, or give up Scripture. It will not suffer us to say that this is an *elect* world, for the "whole world" is *not* elect; and here, the "ours" distinguishes believers from this world, not includes them in it. Propitiation, then, (or atonement—it is the same word,) is for all; and it is the same thing for all: not as actually *availing*, of course, but as fully *available*. It has no limit to its value within the limits of the human race.

Of how that which is available for all avails for any, and how far it avails, I propose to consider in another chapter. Here, I go no farther than this, that the Lord standing in the place of men took the very penalty under which they were,—died, and was made a curse: the value of which must be measured by the infinite value of Him who did this, and the perfection of an obedience so beyond all price.

We are not, therefore, called upon to measure what is measureless, or to conceive of so many sins, or those of so many sinners, weighed out to be atoned for by a particular amount of suffering. Such a commercial idea (as it has been rightly called) of the Lord's wondrous work is an essential degradation of it,—not a high, but a *low* estimate of the requirements of absolute holiness which were to be met thereby. It is not that God must have so much suffering for so much sin, but that His holiness necessitates displeasure proportioned to the evil which awakes it. So even in the final judgment. The deeds done in the body become the manifestation\* of the person upon whom the judgment of God rests correspondingly, but *forever* rests; *not* because, as people have wrongly conceived, the sin itself is necessarily *worthy* of eternal punishment, but because the sinner remains eter-

---

\*" We must all *be manifested* before the judgment-seat of Christ" is the true rendering of 2 Corinthians v. 10.

nally with the character which his life manifests.

The error is therefore plain of making the atonement consist in the endurance of so much agony, as if God could measure out that to the holy Sufferer; whereas, beyond all our conception as was the agony endured, the reality and efficacy of atonement lay in the solemn seal thus put upon the divine estimate of sin, when God's own beloved Son stooped Himself to endure its dreadful penalty.

That He "bare our sins in His own body on the tree," and that God "laid upon Him the iniquity of us all,"—these and such like passages which declare a real imputation of our sins to Christ remain in all their solemn yet precious meaning for us. It was for these sins of ours He suffered, and this suffering of His is that which alone removes them from us, and removes them entirely: how perfectly, we shall see more as we proceed. He was the true Sin-bearer,—our Substitute under penalty, as we have seen. He could not have been this had not our sins been laid on Him; but I turn from this, which will come up before us again, to look at another question in connection with the penalty itself.

In what we have been considering lately, it will be noted that of necessity it would seem it is rather wrath-bearing than death we have been dwelling on; and it may be asked, If all this be true, what part exactly in the penalty has death, then? If wrath could be exhausted by the Lord before dying,—if He could emerge from the darkness into the light, and in peace say once more "Father" before he died,—what need, then, even of dying? Was death for *Him* the wages of sin which He had taken?

And it is undeniable that there has been a tendency two ways, according as one class of texts or the other has been dwelt upon, to make all atonement consist in wrath-bearing, or—far more commonly—all consist in dying. Yet both are plainly unscriptural, as we have sufficiently seen. What we want is to realize the relation of these two parts to each other—to find the due place of each in the Lord's blessed work. We have been looking at the meaning of wrath-bearing of late; and it does raise the necessary question, Why, then, His death? Granting, as we must, the necessity of it according to Scripture, yet why this necessity?

The answer is plain only in the realization of a truth which has been overlooked, conspicuous as it is, by the mass of those who have occupied themselves with the interpretation of Scripture: *the setting aside of the failed first man and the old creation*, to bring in blessing under another head and on another and higher plane altogether.

As already said, the solemnity of death lies in this, that it is the removal of man as failed out of the scene of his failure—the solemn sentence upon him as unfitted for the place for which he was created. The lower creatures, indeed, have never sinned,—are incapable of it,—yet they die; and men plead, therefore, that death is natural. But they cannot persuade themselves, whose whole nature cries out against it. The scriptural account is, "The wages of *sin* is death;" and thus, "man, being in honor, abideth not; he is like the beasts that perish" (Ps. xlix. 12).

Yes, the beasts *do* perish. Intended for nothing but a temporary purpose, they enjoy life while it lasts, without a sorrow for the past or a fear for the future. But man is not a beast: he is the offspring of God, meant to know and enjoy communion with Him forever; and his being leveled to the beasts is the sign of a moral, a spiritual ruin, in which he has forgotten God, and leveled himself to them. He, like them, passes away and is not found; his place knows him no more forever. But not like them, for he has "thoughts" that perish with him, unfulfilled plans and purposes, affections which cling to what they cannot hold, a dread upon his soul which presages a hereafter such as the beast dreads not and desires not, because it has not: "The dust returns to the earth as it was, but the spirit returns to God that gave it."

Such is death for man; and being such, it is the wages of sin. Man in it, as the creature which God made for Adam's paradise, perishes forever,—is set entirely aside. Nor do I forget resurrection when I say so. *Resurrection does not restore him to this.* Job's words are absolutely true here, without bringing in the God-dishonoring thought of annihilation in any wise: "As the cloud is consumed, and vanisheth away, so he that goeth down to the grave shall come up no more: he shall return no more to his house; neither shall his place know him any more." God's grace may give him another and a better thing, but it does not reverse the first judgment.

And thus it is that when the Lord takes death for man He takes it as affirming God's sentence upon man, by which the old creation is set aside forever. Let this be well observed, that whereas the wrath of God upon sin, in being undergone by Christ, is removed (the *effect of atonement is removal*), it is not so with a sentence by which the first man is set aside: if the Lord take this, it must be, *not* to bring him back, but to *affirm his setting aside*. The effect of wrath-bearing is to put away wrath; but the effect of the Lord's dying is that with His death the old creation is confirmed as passing away—is *set aside fully, not restored.*

This is the direct force of 2 Corinthians v. 14-17, not well given in our common version: "For the love of Christ constraineth us; because we thus judge, that if One died for all, *then all died* [or, have died]; and for all He died, that they which live should no longer live unto themselves, but unto Him who died for them and rose again. Wherefore, henceforth know we *no man after the flesh;* yea, though we have known Christ after the flesh, yet now henceforth know we Him no more. Therefore, if any man be in Christ, [it is] *new* creation: old things are passed away; behold, all things are become new."

This is an important passage, and needs attentive consideration. It is a positive statement of the meaning of Christ's death as dying for all,—these "all" being expressly shown not to be limited to "those who live," who are distinguished from them as a class in the latter part of the fourteenth verse.

It is directly affirmed, then, of *all*, that if Christ died for them, *all died*. Our common version has it, "then *were all dead*,"—making it a spiritual state; but the Greek will not admit of this, and the sense also is quite different. The point is as to what Christ's death proves men to have been *under* as sentence, not *in* as state; for He came under our sentence as sinners, but not into our state of sin. He died, then, for all; and so all have died. Before God, the world is judged and passed; as the Lord Himself said of the cross, "Now is the judgment of this world" (Jno. xii. 31). It is not a judgment executed, of course: none could suppose that; but it is a judgment pronounced; and a judgment pronounced is with God as it were executed, so sure and irreversible is it. If Christ, then, died for all, all died. Sentence is not taken away by this, but affirmed.

And this meaning is clearly proved by what follows in Corinthians—"wherefore, henceforth know we *no man after the flesh.*" This is the simple and necessary result (for *faith*, not for sight): if all have died, they are in the flesh no longer; we walk amid a world where men are either alive in Christ or but as it were dead men. But not only so: "yea, though we have known *Christ* after the flesh, yet now henceforth know we Him no more." Even Christ has not taken up again the life which He laid down. He has not returned (that is,) to His former state upon earth. That is over; and the Christ we know is One who is in resurrection in the glory of God. An immeasurably higher condition, you say. Surely it is; but the former one is passed away, and passed away in that which affirmed God's sentence upon it. Where, then, are we who *live?* In Christ; and "if any man be in Christ, it is *new* creation: old things are passed away; behold, all things are become new."

Thus the sense of the passage is plain and perspicuous. And the meaning of the Lord's taking of death is very clearly set forth. Atonement does not restore the old Adam condition, but affirms its judgment and setting aside. For those saved by it, the darkness of distance from God who is light is passed with the darkness upon the cross. It is thus the gospel of Luke, which gives especially the effects of the work of Christ for the conscience, connects them: "And it was about the sixth hour; and there was darkness over all the land until the ninth hour; and the sun was darkened, and *the vail of the temple was rent in the midst.*" The vail *meant* darkness, as that in which God dwelled for man; its rending means that "God is in the light" (1 Jno. i. 7).

But with His *death* the apostle Matthew takes especial care to connect what in fact did not occur till after His resurrection: "And the earth did quake, and the rocks rent, and the graves were opened, and many bodies of the saints which slept arose, and came out of the graves after His resurrection, and went into the holy city, and appeared unto many." The answer to His death is resurrection; not the recommencement of the old Adam life, which is finally and forever set aside.

Thus those alive in Christ are dead with Him also, and as it is specifically stated, "dead to sin," "dead to law," "dead to the elements of the world" —to all that makes it up,—and "not in the flesh." But to that we must return hereafter: our present subject closes here.

## Chapter XXIV.

### *Redemption and Atonement.*

WE now come to look at the efficacy of atonement—that is to say, its connection with redemption. For redemption is not, in Scripture, what it is for many, a thing accomplished for the whole world. No passage which hints at this even can be produced from the Word. Redemption was, for Israel, the breaking of Pharaoh's yoke. The redemption of our body is accomplished in resurrection (Rom. viii. 23). "We have redemption through His blood, the forgiveness of sins, according to the riches of His grace" (Eph. i. 7). Such statements sufficiently show us that redemption is an accomplished deliverance,—that it involves, not a salvable state, but a *salvation*, which the world as a whole never knows. And redemption is "through His blood" shed in atonement: it is that in which the proper efficacy of atonement is declared. "Not redeemed with corruptible things, as silver and gold, . . . . but with the precious blood of Christ, as of a lamb without blemish and without spot" (1 Pet. i. 18, 19).

A difficulty which has divided Christians comes in here. If redemption is by atonement, and atonement—the "propitiation" of 1 John ii. 2,—is for the whole world, how is it that in fact all are not redeemed? The answer to which is given by some that atonement is only conditionally efficacious, and this is plainly the only possible one if such texts as that just cited are accepted in their natural sense. The alternative is only to explain, as all strict Calvinists do, the "world," as simply the *elect* among Jews and Gentiles. But this is not what "the whole world" means. What would the very persons who urge this think, if when the same apostle in the same epistle says, "We know that we are of God, and the *whole world* lieth in wickedness," a similar limitation were maintained? "We" and "the whole world" are no more contrasted in the one case than "ours" and "of the whole world" are in the other. Or again when Paul declares that "whatsoever the law saith it saith to them that are under the law, that every mouth might be stopped, and the *whole world* become guilty before God," if it were contended that this meant anything less than all men, who would admit it?

Take 1 Tim. ii. 1–6 as another statement. Prayer is enjoined for all men, for God our Saviour "will have *all men* to be saved, and to come to the knowledge of the truth; for there is one God, and one Mediator between God and men, the Man Christ Jesus, who gave Himself a *ransom for all*, to be testified in due time." Here, the "all men" must be consistently interpreted throughout.

So the gospel which Paul preached to the Corinthians was that "Christ died for our sins" (1 Cor. xv. 3), as the doctrine of his second epistle is that "He died for all" (v. 14). Only on this ground, indeed, could the gospel be sent out, as it confessedly is, to "every creature," or could it be spoken of as "the grace of God which bringeth salvation to all" (Tit. ii. 11).

Only a provision actually made for all could

fulfill the fair meaning of such texts as these· and we may not bring into them any doctrine oi election, to limit them. They are the testimony of the desire of God's heart for all. They are the assurance that if men die unsaved, the responsibility of their ruin is with themselves alone. They are the encouragement to implicit confidence in a love that welcomes, and has title to welcome, all who come by Christ to God.

But while these texts seem very clear, and the sufficiency and applicability of the atonement are in words allowed by some who contest even the meaning of them, there are others which to many occasion difficulty in regard to a "propitiation for the sins of the whole world." These are the texts which speak of substitution in the strict sense.

Substitution is not found as a term in Scripture, but the *fact* of it is abundantly found. Every victim whose blood was shed in atonement for the sin of him who offered it was a real substitute for the offerer. It has been objected that the word for "substitution" does not occur in connection with the Levitical sacrifices or the Lord's work; but that the "Son of Man came to give His life a ransom for [ἀντὶ—instead of] many" is said in both Matthew and Mark, while in 1 Tim. ii. 6 we have the word ἀντίλυτρον—a ransom-price. But, as I have said, the doctrine is there where the term is not. If the Lord were "made a curse for us," how could this be but as representing us? If He "bare our sins in His own body on the tree," what else was this but substitution? And there is much of similar language elsewhere, as we shall see. In fact, the difficulty of which I have spoken arises from the way in which it is every-where pressed that our Lord's work for us was of true substitutionary character.

For while, in a certain sense, the Lord might be said to be a ransom in place of all, it is evident that where faith is not and while it is not the ransom is as if it were not. And there are expressions thus as to the sacrifice which to faith and only faith could apply. Take one from Isaiah liii: "The Lord hath laid on Him the iniquity of us all." Here, faith speaks, and the words are surely not true of any other than believers. But then comes the difficulty: was there, then, when Christ died, some special work needed and undergone for the sins of believers?

The same question might be asked, perhaps even more pointedly, with regard to 1 Pet. ii. 24: "Who Himself bare our sins in His own body on the tree." For this "bearing" surely speaks of the removal of them from before God's sight. Would it be possible, then, to say of the world that He bare *their* sins in His body on the tree? Surely not, or they would most certainly be saved. He could not have borne their sins and they yet have to bear them. A strict and proper substitution assuredly necessitates the removal of responsibility from the one for whom the substitute assumes it. It results, therefore, that a substitute for the world the Lord was not.

And the language of Scripture is every-where in accord with this. It does speak of propitiation for the sins of the whole world: it does *not* speak of their sins being "laid on" or "borne" by Christ. These two things have been confounded on the one hand, and made into a doctrine of limited atonement, or of substitution for all. On the other, where the distinction has been noticed, it has been taken to imply that on the cross there was a work for all and a *special* work for the elect beside—a double atonement, as it were; that it was a propitiation for all, a substitution for the elect. In other words, the Arminian atonement and the Calvinistic atonement are both considered true, and to be found together in the work of Christ. But this leads to much confusion and misreading of Scripture, much manifest opposition to it.

It has led some to speak of salvation as a thing wrought out eighteen hundred years ago,—not simply the blessed work which saves, but actual salvation. Faith serves as a telescope to see what existed before we saw it, and what it had nothing to do therefore with producing. The sins of believers were thus dealt with and removed before they were committed, and people find peace by faith, but are not justified by it. All this is in complete opposition to the Word; yet it is a just consequence of the doctrine of a substitution for the elect, and their sins borne when the Lord Jesus died.

Yet He did bear their sins upon the tree, and Jehovah laid on Him the iniquity of us all. "Ours"? Whose, then? and how does this differ from the doctrine just repudiated? The answer is very simple. These words are the language of faith,—of believers; and of believers as such only is it true. He bare the sins of believers on the tree, and this is equivalent to what we have been saying—that the efficacy of atonement is conditional. It is conditioned upon faith, and His bearing the sins of *believers* is a complete negative of universalism in all its phases. Only their sins are *borne*, although the atonement is for the sins of the whole world; and the duty and responsibility of faith are therefore to be pressed on every creature. The sins of believers were really borne eighteen hundred years ago; but only when men become believers are their sins borne, therefore. The very man who to-day believes, and whose sins were borne eighteen hundred years ago, not only could not *say* yesterday that his sins were borne, but they were really *not* borne yesterday, although the work was done eighteen hundred years ago. But it was done for *believers*, and only to-day is he a believer. The work of atonement only now has its proper efficacy for him: he is justified by faith.

All this is perfectly simple. It is transparently so, indeed. What has clouded and disfigured it? On the one hand, the importing into it the doctrine of election, which is never done in Scripture; on the other, the thought that our iniquity being laid upon the Lord meant the putting away of so much sin for so much suffering,—so many actual sins of just so many persons being provided for, and no other. But this would make propitiation for the world impossible, and destroy, as we have seen, if consistently followed out, justification by faith. The simple meaning of the texts appealed to involves no such difficulty.

The Lord Jesus, then, was the Substitute for believers, and thus made propitiation for the sins of the world, its efficacy being conditioned upon faith. He stood as the Representative of a class, not a fixed number of individuals,—of a people to whom men are invited and besought to join themselves, the value of the atonement being more than sufficient and available for all who come. The responsibility of coming really rests, where Scrip- always places it, upon men themselves.

## ATONEMENT. 193

Now, if it be asked, What is the issue of this invitation? Do any become of the number of His people really except in virtue of a divine work wrought sovereignly in their souls? it is true, none do so. "To as many as received Him, to them gave He right to become children of God, even to those who believe in His name; which were born, not of blood, nor of the will of the flesh, nor of the will of man, but of God" (Jno. i. 12, 13). Such is the decisive statement of Scripture. Men are born again to be children of God; and the new birth is not of man's will: the moment we speak of it, we speak of that which assures us that man's will is wholly adverse. For to be born again is never a thing put upon man as what he is responsible for: it is, in its very nature, outside of this. And "Ye must be born again" is the distinct affirmation that on the ground of responsibility all is over. "How often would I . . . ! and ye would not," is the Lord's lament over Israel; and it is true of man in nature everywhere. Terrible it is to realize it, but it is true.

Man is bidden to repent and believe the gospel. There is no lack of abundant evidence. It is the condemnation, that "light is come into the world, and men *loved* darkness rather than light, because their deeds were evil." They refuse the evidence that convicts them, and refuse the grace that would save them. "As in water face answereth to face, so the heart of man to man." That he needs to be born again shows that God must work sovereignly, or the whole world perish. So it is quickening from the dead and new creation. These terms all witness to the utter ruin of man, as they do to the omnipotent grace of God in conversion.

These terms speak all of a new life conferred, and with this life the condition required in order to efficacious atonement is accomplished; there is "justification *of life*" (Rom. v. 18)—justification attaching to the life possessed. The last Adam is made a quickening Spirit (1 Cor. xv. 45), after havgone down to death and come up out of it; and the life He gives brings those who receive it into a new creation, of which He is the Representative-Head. To these He is Kinsman-Redeemer, according to the type (Lev. xxv. 48). The new relationship is their security and entrance into full blessing, to which His work is now their absolute title.

It is here that election does come in; not to limit the provision, nor to restrict in any wise the grace that bids and welcomes all, but to secure the blessing of those who otherwise would refuse and forfeit it as the rest do. The grace to all is not narrowed by the "grace upon grace" to many. The universal offer means and is based on a universal provision, and a provision of exactly the same character for all alike, in which God testifies that He hath "no pleasure in the death of him that dieth," but "will have all men to be saved, and to come to the knowledge of the truth." It may be asked, as it has been asked, Of what avail is a provision for all which saves not one additional to the elect number? The answer which Scripture would give is, "What if some did not believe? shall their unbelief make the faith [or faithfulness] of God without effect? God forbid." The salvation of men is from God; the damnation of men is from themselves. This all the pleadings, warnings, offers of God affirm. And grace refused is still grace, and to be proclaimed to His praise.

The last Adam is thus the Representative-Head of His people, as in His atoning work He was their Substitute before God. "Upon the seed of Abraham"—that is, believers,—"He layeth hold." This affirms the work to be for all, conditionally upon faith; and for believers *un*conditionally. "The righteousness of God is by faith of Jesus Christ unto all; and upon"—or "over," rather, as a shield or sheltering roof,—"all them that believe."

## Chapter XXV.

*Resurrection the Sign of Complete Atonement.*

FOR the great mass of Christians, the resurrection of Christ has dropped out of the place in reference to atonement which it finds in Scripture. The resurrection side of the gospel has dropped out. Yet God has been graciously reviving the truth of it in many hearts. Let us seek to get hold of what is wrapped up for us in the joyful tidings of Christ risen from the dead.

"If Christ be not risen," says the apostle to the Corinthians, "ye are yet in your sins." The resurrection was the full, open acceptance of the work which alone could put them away. It was God manifesting Himself on the side of those for whom the work was now accomplished. Hence faith rests in "Him who raised up Jesus our Lord from the dead;" and it is added, in explanation of this, "who was delivered for our offenses, and raised again *for our justification*" (Rom. iv. 24, 25).

"Resurrection *from* the dead" has always this character of acceptance of the one raised up, and must not be confounded with the simple fact of resurrection in itself. When the Lord, at the Mount of Transfiguration, "charged them that they should tell no man what things they had seen until the Son of Man were risen from the dead," the disciples "kept that saying with themselves, questioning one with another what the rising from the dead should mean" (Mark ix. 9, 10). Familiar as they were with the general truth that the dead should rise, this rising *from* the dead—not from the *state* of the dead, but from among the dead themselves, a special resurrection which would leave the rest unchanged,—was to them a new and unknown thing. "I know that he shall rise in the resurrection at the last day," Martha's words as to her brother, was the expression of the faith of every orthodox Jew of that day. Alas! even yet, the general faith of christendom goes no further. But the Lord, in arguing with the Sadducees, speaks of a special class, "those who should be accounted *worthy to attain* that world and *the resurrection from the dead*," as "the children of God, *being* the children of the resurrection" (Luke xx. 35, 36). The resurrection from the dead approves as accepted of God all that participate in it. Thus is it pre-eminently, then, with the resurrection of Christ from the dead. It is the triumphant demonstration, in the face of His enemies, of God for Him whom they had crucified and slain. "What sign showest Thou," said the Jews once to Him, "seeing that Thou doest these things?" and the Lord answers, "'Destroy this temple, and in three days I will raise it up.' .... He spake of the temple of His body" (Jno. ii. 19, 21).

All through His ministry among men indeed the signs of the Father's approval and delight were openly given. The works which He did in His Father's name bore witness to Him. The Father's voice and the descending Spirit had borne witness also. But these were personal to Himself alone. Now, having completed His work on behalf of others, His resurrection becomes the seal of the acceptance of what was done in their behalf. It is the testimony still of the approval of His own personal perfection, but as standing in a place altogether apart from what was His due personally, and where the holiness of God tested Him as the fire of the altar the sacrifice upon it. In result, all the sweet savor of the sacrifice was brought out by it.

So of the Lord, as had long ago been declared by another prophetically personating Him, "Thou wilt not leave my soul in hell [or "hades"], neither wilt Thou suffer Thy Holy One to see corruption." It was as the *Holy One* He could not see it. "Who in the days of His flesh, when He had offered up prayers and supplications, with strong crying and tears, unto Him that was able to save Him *out of* death,"—not, as in the common version, "*from* death,"—"and was heard in that He feared," or as in the margin, "for His piety" (Heb. v. 7). It was this upon which all depended, what under the most perfect, most bitter trial, was found in Him. The white linen garments of the high-priest, the type of spotless righteousness wrought out, were the only ones, as we have elsewhere seen, in which he could enter the most holy place. Nothing else but such righteousness could bring Him in there, the representative of a people accepted in Him.

The declaration of this acceptance waited not, indeed, for resurrection. His testimony before He dies is that the atoning work is "finished" (Jno. xix. 30). He had no sooner died than the rent vail declared it. And the threefold witness of the Spirit, water, and blood answered at once the thrust of the soldier's spear (Jno. xix. 34, 35; 1 Jno. v. 8). Already the record is, that "God hath given to us eternal life, and this life is in His Son" (1 Jno. v. 11). It is only in continuance of these testimonies that by the glory of the Father He is raised from among the dead, and then in due season "by His own blood He entered in once into the holy place, having obtained eternal redemption" (Heb. ix. 12).

Blessed it is to see the promptitude of this utterance of the heart of God as to that which is in His sight of such infinite value. At once the rent vail attests that the "merciful and faithful High-Priest" has made "propitiation for the sins of the people" (chap. ii. 17). The *typical* blood must wait until the high-priest himself has entered the sanctuary; but not so the antitypical. The vail could not have been rent had not the mercy-seat been already sprinkled. The typical blood was but the blood of bulls and goats, and required human hands to carry it in; the antitypical needed none such to present it to the omniscient eye of Him to whom it was offered. The difference is one of those suited necessary contrasts between figure and reality, of which there are so many, and which constitute one of the gravest admonitions to caution in the application of the figures.

That it is the *high-priest* who makes "atonement in the holy place" (Lev. xvi. 17), and of whom the apostle speaks in the interpretation, Heb. ii. 10, is indeed a difficulty with those who having learned from Scripture that "if He were on earth, He should not be a priest" (chap. viii. 4) suppose therefore that at the cross He was not. The mistake is natural, but the Word of God meets the difficulty for us in the words of the Saviour as to this, "I, if I be *lifted up from* the earth." At the cross He was no more "on earth," and this is no strain of an expression: He had in fact done with earth,—was passing from it, His place among men gone. And here, of necessity, His priesthood began; else was there no priestly offering up at all, for assuredly it was not in resurrection that the altar-fire consumed the victim; and the ministry of the altar was exclusively the priest's work. Thus, surely, it is clear how it was our High-Priest who as such made atonement, as it is also clear by the rent vail and the resurrection itself that *before* resurrection the blood was sprinkled on the heavenly mercy-seat.

Resurrection followed on the third day to set the Second Man in His Last-Adam place. It is plain how 1 Corinthians xv. connects this place with the "spiritual body" of the resurrection. "There is a natural body, and there is a spiritual body. And so it is written, The first man Adam was made a living soul; the last Adam was made a quickening spirit." The first Adam is plainly himself a living soul with a natural body,—the word "natural" being here the adjective of the word "soul" itself, a body fitted for the soul, as we may say. The last Adam is the pattern of those of His heavenly race, as the first was of his earthy race. Only they are not yet in the image of the heavenly, (as they shall be,) though they are heavenly; and the Lord too is not merely a *living* spirit, but, according to His own necessary pre-eminence, a life-*giving* spirit. This is so beautifully pictured in the scene in the twentieth of John, where as God breathed into Adam at the first, *He* breathes now upon His disciples, that I do not doubt it to be the meaning there. He has taken and is representing to us His last-Adam place. But this I do not dwell on further here.

He rises, then, with a spiritual body,—does not assume it afterward, as some have thought. The wounds in His hands and side, which some have brought forward to prove the opposite, do as little prove it as Zechariah xii. 10 or xiii. 6 would prove it of a day yet future. Return to His former condition before the cross we have seen He could not. His death means the acceptance of the solemn sentence by which man as first created had been set aside out of .his place. Restore this He does not; while He can and does bring in for His people what is infinitely better.

He rises, then, the Representative of His people in their new place of unchanging blessing, in the likeness to which they are to be conformed. He is raised again for the justification of all believers. For *these* His death has *absolutely* atoned, for these acceptance is complete and unconditional; while individually every one comes into it by faith,—is justified by faith. Here is the one condition upon which Scripture uniformly insists, in regard to propitiation no less than substitution: for, be it that He is a propitiation for the sins of the whole world, this is *not* unconditionally; He is a "propitiation by faith in His blood," as the common version, or "a propitiation through faith by His blood," as the Revised Version better renders it. The door is indeed open to all the world, but those who enter enter by faith; and only thus is the propitiation really theirs.

The resurrection of Christ is therefore God coming out openly for His people, and Christ risen is the measure of their acceptance. His is theirs. He is acccpted for them; they are accepted in Him. *Substitution* ends with the cross, for our place in which He stood ends there; but *representation* does not end with the cross, but the place He takes in resurrection He brings us into. We are dead with Him is the language of Scripture; we are risen also with Him: we are "accepted"—"taken into favor;" "*graced*," if we may use the literal word,—"in the Beloved."

His place is ours; only we must remember that when we say this, we limit it strictly to that of which we are speaking—His place in resurrection. There are glories, it need hardly be said, that are entirely His own,—not only *divine* glories, but as man also. We speak simply now of a *place of acceptance as manifested in resurrection from the dead;* not even as yet of the opened heavens: for when we go so far, we have to remember that not all accepted ones go even to heaven. There will be by and by a new *earth* also, in which dwelleth righteousness. But so far as we have reached, we speak of what is the common portion of saints of all ages, heavenly and earthly alike. In this sense, then, we say His death is ours, His resurrection is ours, His acceptance is ours: we are accepted and find our place in Him; *we are identified with Him.*

## Chapter XXVI.

### *Union and Identification with Christ.*

AT this point it becomes necessary to consider the nature of union with Christ, and to distinguish it from what has been confounded with it, though very different,—identification with Him. Scripture, indeed, which speaks of being joined or united to Christ, does not use the latter term; but the equivalent is abundantly given in the New Testament in the expression with which our last chapter closed—"in Christ." This is taken by most Christians as the very term for union. We must look, therefore, the more carefully into the matter.

Identification may also, and will, be in certain respects the result of union. Husband and wife become thus "one flesh;" "he that is joined to the Lord is one spirit" (1 Cor. vi. 17). Here is, no doubt the origin of the confusion; but it is none the less such. We may speak of identification where there could not be union. We are identified with Christ in His death, not united to Him in it; identified in nature with Him, not united to His nature; identified with Him as our Representative before God, not united with Him as such.

These things are not in fact for us the result of union. "If any man be in Christ, [it is] new creation," says the apostle (2 Cor. v. 17). That is what "in Christ" means—a new creation. At new birth there is dropped into the soul the seed of divine, eternal life. It is not, as so many think, merely a moral change which is effected; but just as that which is born of the flesh is flesh, so that which is born of the Spirit is spirit. Those so born are truly partakers of His nature, and thus not simply adopted but real children of God. Christ is their life, the new "Adam" of a new creation; but in which He is Creator as well as Head, as we have seen.*

But union is never said to be by or in new creation, but accomplished in a very different way. "He that is joined to the Lord is one spirit;" and the context shows that it is of marriage the apostle is speaking: "For two, saith He, shall be one flesh; but he that is united to the Lord is one spirit." Such a figure is not and could not be applied to new creation. The Creator is not united to the creature, nor the parent to the child; but the head is united to the body, the husband to the wife, and the apostle in Eph. v. 25-33 applies both these as illustrative of the Church's relationship to Christ. A man's wife is his own flesh, his body: and "no man ever yet hated his own flesh, but nourisheth and cherisheth it, even as Christ the Church; for we are members of His body."

To be of the last Adam's race and to be members of Christ are in Scripture perfectly distinct

---

*It is important to see clearly the exact force of this term "creation," as Scripture uses it. In Genesis i., in the divine work, we have the creation of heaven and earth, of the living soul (the animal), and of man. All else is said to be *made*, and not created. The creation of heaven and earth speaks, of course, of their first origination; but in the case of the beast the soul, in that of the man the spirit, are the successive additions, which justify the term "creation" as applied to them. The beast has a soul (Gen. i. 30), but not a spirit. Man has not only a soul, but a spirit also (1 Thess. v. 23), by virtue of which alone he has the knowledge of a man (1 Cor. ii. 11), and is the offspring of God (Acts xvii. 28; Heb. xii. 9). Yet the beast and the man are said to be "created," and not the soul and spirit only. So the child of God, by this new spiritual life communicated at new birth, becomes "a new creation."

things, though in the minds of many there is sad confusion again as to this. Many belong and will yet belong to the new creation who never belong to the body of Christ at all. We are *baptized* by the Spirit into the body of Christ (1 Cor. xii. 13); and that baptism began only at Pentecost (Acts i. 5; Matt. iii. 11); while the Church will be complete at the coming of Christ, before the thousand years begin of the earth's blessing. But to pursue this would lead us too far from our present subject. It is enough to say that those baptized at Pentecost into the body of Christ were already before this born again and a new creation. And if these things were thus distinct in them, they must be as much so in all others.

"In Christ" is not, then, union; it is identification by virtue of that new life which is received when we are born again, and which connects us with the last Adam our Representative Head. This identification is twofold: first, in the new, divine nature received, so that it can be said, "For both He that sanctifieth and they who are sanctified are all *of one;* for which cause He is not ashamed to call them brethren" (Heb. ii. 11); while secondly, we are identified with Him in the work He has accomplished for us as our Representative. The identification with Him in nature is what is needed to constitute true representation:—"Behold I and the children which God hath given Me; forasmuch, then, as the children are partakers of flesh and blood, He also Himself likewise took part in the same; that through death He might destroy him that had the power of death, and deliver those who all their lifetime, through fear of death, were subject to bondage; for verily He taketh not hold of angels, but of the seed of Abraham He taketh hold" (Heb. ii. 13-16).

We have seen how this death of Christ for His people—because all are truly welcome to become His people—becomes a propitiation for the whole world. A true basis for representation is found in this true brotherhood between the Lord and His own, without narrowing the limits of an atonement for all.

But thus too the various views of ritualists and others based upon the Lord's supposed union with all men in His assumption of the common humanity are completely set aside. Without contending further as to the Scripture thought of "union," it is not a common humanity which establishes relationship between the Lord and the whole race of men. It is by what is in men the *new* nature, not the old, that they become His "brethren." And the new life that they thus receive is, as His own words testify, a life which is the fruit of His death alone: "Except a corn of wheat fall into the ground and die, it abideth alone; but if it die, it bringeth forth much fruit." This He says of His own death and its results. But for His death, His perfect, spotless manhood could have availed nothing for us. Our link is with Him the other side of death, a death by which the first man and the old creation are set aside forever. Identification and union are both for us with Him risen from the dead.

It is for want of understanding this that the force of the apostle's words in Romans v. 10 is so little seen: "If when we were enemies we were reconciled to God by the death of His Son, much more, being reconciled, we shall be saved through His life." "Who was delivered for our offenses," he says in the fourth chapter, "and raised again for our justification." Thus it is His risen life that is salvation for us; *not* simply because "He ever liveth to make intercession for us," but because that life is the new beginning of every thing for us. The death and resurrection of Christ are thus the pillars of the gospel: His death the knife to cut the fatal link of connection with the old fallen head; His resurrection the power that lifts us into the new place of acceptance and the eternal joy. Dead with Christ, we are dead to sin (Rom. vi. 11), to the law (chap. vii. 4), and to the elements of the world, and are no longer alive in it (Col. ii. 20). We are not of the world, even as Christ is not (Jno. xvii. 16).

From this it results that "in Christ Jesus neither circumcision availeth any thing, nor uncircumcision,"—neither the Jewish nor the Gentile footing, —"but new creation." And here is the practical rule of Christianity; "and as many as walk according to *this rule*, peace be on them, and mercy" (Gal. vi. 15, 16).

How important, then, in every way is this resurrection side of the gospel! Alike for full deliverance and for a true Christian walk it must be known. Except as dead with Christ, I have no *title* to reckon myself dead to sin: for this is not feeling or finding, not experience at all, but faith; and faith which not only sees that Christ has borne my *sins*, but that He has stood for *me*, in my stead, so that His death has removed me and all the evil of my evil nature forever out of the sight of God, to give me my true self now in Christ in His presence. I am delivered from legal self-occupation, the enemy of all true holiness, and enabled for occupation with Christ, the true secret of holiness and of power. "We all with open face beholding the glory of the Lord are changed into His image, from glory to glory, even as by the Lord the Spirit." The imprint of this glory it is by which we become the letter of commendation of Christ read and known of all men; a letter written, not with ink, but by the Spirit of the living God; not on tables of stone, but on fleshy tables of the heart (2 Cor. iii. 18, 3).

Upon all this I must not here dwell; and it has been dwelt upon at length by many. But it shows how in every detail of it the doctrine of atonement connects with all Christian experience and practice together. May its rich and blessed fruits be found in us as in him who said, "The life which I now live in the flesh I live by the faith of the Son of God, who loved me, and gave Himself for me."

## Chapter XXVII.

### *God Glorified and Glorifying Himself.*

WE have seen the work of atonement as a work needed by man, applicable and applied to him for his complete justification and deliverance. And this involves, as we have seen, God's satisfaction with the blessed work done on man's behalf, of which the rent vail and the resurrection are the prompt witnesses on His part. But we have reserved to this place, as the fittest for it, the full divine side of the cross, so far as we can utter it. In our review of Scripture, it has necessarily often occupied us; but in this sketch of the doctrine—now very near conclusion,—it needs to be afresh considered and put in connection with it. It is indeed, and must be, the crowning glory of the whole.

We begin, naturally and necessarily, with that which meets our need as sinners, and yet even so that need is never rightly met until we have seen, not merely our sins put away, but whose hand it is that does this. Nor must we stop here even with *Christ* for us. It must be "*God* for us." "Lord, show us the Father, and it sufficeth us."

Quite true, if we have come to Christ we have come to the Father; if we know Christ we know the Father: and so our Lord replies to Philip's words which we have just quoted. But we need to understand this. It is no long road to travel, from the Son to the Father. The Father is perfectly and only revealed in the Son. Yet many stop short of this for long; using Christ's work more as a shelter *from* God than a way *to* God: like Israel on that night in Egypt when God says, "When I see the blood, I will pass over you;" but how different from the Psalmist's deeper utterance —"*Thou* art my hiding-place." To be hidden *from* God, or hidden *in* God—which is our faith's experience, reader?

It is evident that in these two thoughts God is in contrasted characters: to pass from one to the other involves a revelation. And as Philip's words truly say, nothing but this last suffices the heart. God has made it for Himself: nothing but Himself will satisfy it.

It is true "the Son of Man must be lifted up:" here is a *necessity*. Yes, but "God so loved the world, that He gave His only begotten Son:" here is God Himself revealed. It is the cross in each case that is contemplated, but how differently! And it is this divine side of the cross that is now to occupy us.

God *glorifies* Himself in *revealing* Himself. He shines out. Clouds and darkness no more encompass Him. He is in the light, and in Him is no darkness at all.

And we, blessed be His name! are in the light. The darkness is passing, if not wholly passed. The true light already shines. Through the rent vail of the flesh of Jesus the divine glory shines. It is of His cross our precious Redeemer says, "Now is the Son of Man glorified, and God is glorified in Him; if God be glorified in Him, God will also glorify Him in Himself, and will straightway glorify Him." These words may well serve as the text of all we have to say.

"Now is the Son of Man glorified." No ray of glory shone *upon* Him: all was deepest darkness, profoundest humiliation; yet in the cross the Son of Man was glorified. Well might He say to Peter, "Whither I go, thou canst not follow Me now." Who but Himself could have gone down into the abyss where was no standing, to lay again the misplaced foundations of the earth? Who but He could have borne the awful trial of the fire of divine holiness, searching out all the inward parts, and in that place have been but a sweet savor to an absolutely holy God? Who but He could have assumed those sins of ours which He calls in the prophetic psalms "My sins," and risen up again, not merely in the might of a divine person, but in the power of a thoroughly human righteousness?

Yes, verily, "the Son of Man was glorified;" but more—"*God* is glorified in Him." There are two ways in which we may look at this.

First: God was glorified by the perfect obedience of One who owed no obedience, as He had done no wrong. He restored what He took not away. He confessed fully a sin He had Himself to measure in infinite suffering and alone. He confessed and proclaimed a righteousness and holiness in God to which He surrendered Himself, vindicating it against Himself when God forsook Him as the bearer of sin. And He presented to God a perfect humanity, fully tried and beyond question, in which the fall was retrieved, and God's thought in man's creation brought out and cleared from the dishonor the first man had cast upon it. And goodness triumphed in weakness over evil; the bruised foot of the woman's seed trod down the serpent's head.

But secondly: when we think of the mystery of His person, it is God Himself who has taken—truly taken—this earthen vessel of a pure and true humanity, that He might give to *Himself* the atonement for man's sin. It is *God* who has coveted and gained capacity for weakness, suffering, and death itself, that He might demonstrate eternal holiness, and yet manifest everlasting love to men. It is God who has "devised means that His banished should not be expelled from Him." And it is God who has cleared up all the darkness of this world by this great joy found at the bottom of a cup of awful agony; who has brought out of the eater meat, out of the strong sweetness, out of death and the grave eternal life!

It is this revelation of God in the cross that is its moral power. In all that He does, the Son of God is doing the Father's will, keeping the Father's commandments, making known the Father's name. The gospel is the "gospel of God"—His good news,—in which "glory to God in the highest" coalesces with "peace on earth, delight in men." And so it is "I, if I be lifted up from the earth, will draw all men unto Me." Every way it becomes true, "when we were enemies, we were reconciled to God through the death of His Son." This is that moral power of the cross which some would make the whole matter, but which can only be when found in a true atonement for our sins. Mere exhibition would be theatrical, not real, and could not do the work designed in it. A real need really met, a just debt paid at personal cost, guilt measured only and removed by such a sacrifice,—this alone can lay hold upon the heart so as to be of abiding control over it. And this *does* control: "O

Lord, truly I am Thy servant; I am Thy servant and the son of Thine handmaid; *Thou hast loosed my bonds.*"

But the moral effect of the cross, the power of the display of divine glory in it, is not to be measured merely by what it accomplishes among men. Scripture has shown to us, clearly if not in its full extent, a sphere which is far more extensive than that of redemption. Into the "sufferings of Christ and the glories which should follow," says the apostle Peter, "the angels desire to look." And while by it the Redeemer, "gone up on high," has "led captivity captive," and "having spoiled principalities and powers, made a show of them openly, triumphing over them in it,"—on the other hand, "God, who is rich in mercy, for His great love wherewith He loved us, even when we were dead in sins, hath quickened us together with Christ, and raised us up together, and made us sit together in heavenly places in Christ Jesus; that in the ages to come He might show the exceeding riches of His grace in His kindness toward us in Christ Jesus." And more precisely the same apostle speaks of God's "intent that now *unto the principalities and powers in heavenly places* might be known through the Church the manifold wisdom of God." (Eph. ii. 4–7; iii. 10.)

Not to us only, nor only for our sakes, is the glory of God revealed! Would He hide from others the glorious face which has shone upon us? On the contrary, if "the Lamb" be "the light of" the heavenly city of the redeemed, the light of the city itself is "like unto a stone most precious, even like a jasper stone, clear as crystal;" for He that sits upon the throne is "like a *jasper* and a sardine stone," and the city has the glory of God (Rev. iv. 3; xxi. 11). "Unto Him," says the apostle, "be glory *in the Church,* in Christ Jesus, through all generations of the age of ages" (Eph. iii. 21).

God, then, being glorified in Christ, glorifies Him in Himself, giving Him a name above every name. "By His own blood He enters in once into the holy place, having obtained eternal redemption" (Heb. ix. 12). Not simply as the divine Person that He always was does He enter there, but now as the One who has by Himself purged sins He sits down at the right hand of the Majesty on high (chap. i. 3). He is Head over all things, Head of all principality and power, Head to the Church which is His body (Col. i. 18; ii. 10; Eph. i. 22). His request is fulfilled: "Father, glorify Thy Son," and the end in which His heart rests He names, "that Thy Son also may glorify Thee" (Jno. xvii. 2).

The end and object of all is the glory of God. It is perfectly, divinely true, that "God hath ordained for His own glory whatsoever comes to pass." In order to guard this from all possibility of mistake, we have only to remember who is this God, and what the glory that He seeks. It is He who is the God and Father of our Lord Jesus Christ,—of Him in whom divine love came seeking *not* her own, among us as "One that serveth." It is He who, sufficient to Himself, can receive no real accession of glory from His creatures, but from whom— "Love," as He is "Light,"—cometh down every good and every perfect gift, in whom is no variableness nor shadow of turning. Of His own alone can His creatures give to Him.

The glory of such an one is found in the display of His own goodness, righteousness, holiness, truth;

in manifesting Himself as in Christ He has manifested Himself and will forever. The glory of this God is what of necessity all things must serve,—adversaries and evil as well as all else. He has ordained it; His power will insure it; and when all apparent clouds and obstructions are removed, then shall He rest—"rest in His love" forever, although eternity only will suffice for the apprehension of the revelation. "God shall be all in all" gives in six words the ineffable result.

Christ, then, is the One in whom God has revealed and glorified Himself—glorified by revealing Himself. Upon Him all the ages wait: "all things were created by Him and for Him." He is the "Father of eternity:" Head of the Church His body; last Adam of a new creation.

And in this eternal purpose of God we have our place, therefore, and how blessed an one!—"chosen in Him before the foundation of the world, that we should be holy and without blame before Him in love" (Eph. i. 4). "That in the ages to come He might show forth the exceeding riches of His grace in His kindness toward us in Christ Jesus"—"God, for His great love wherewith He loved us, even when we were dead in sins, hath quickened us together with Christ; and hath raised us up together, and made us sit together in heavenly places in Christ Jesus."

The cross of Christ was an absolute necessity for the salvation of men; but it is more,—it is an absolute necessity for the fulfillment of God's eternal purpose to show forth the exceeding riches of His grace. In it already has been accomplished that which is the wonder and joy of heaven, the fullest song on the lips of her adoring worshipers. But the grace in this must have full expression—the fullest. He who has become a man for our salvation cannot give up again the manhood He has assumed. Service is the fruit of love. He has taken the place of service, and will keep it: the love is not temporary, but eternal, in His heart; the expression of it should be as eternal as the love.

And if He come down to this place, and as man lead the praises of His people, men must be in the nearest place to Him; that it may be, not merely compassion seen in Him, but love; and love, free, unearned, divine, the exceeding riches of the grace of God.

Thus, too, the cross is honored, exalted, lifted up before the eyes of all the universe. That He died; for what He died; how gloriously the work has been achieved. While the arms that thus are thrown around men encircle all: for it is God in Christ who has done this, and who *is* this,—God, the God and Father of all.

There are various circles and ranks among the redeemed in glory. There are earthly and heavenly, and differences too among these. This of course implies no difference in justification, in the atonement made alike for all. A common salvation has been taken generally to mean a common place for every one of the saved; and the special place and privileges of the body of Christ have been assumed to belong to all of these. But Scripture is as plain as need be that this is not so. There will be, of those whose names are written in heaven, a church of first-born ones, as there will be a company of "spirits of just men made perfect"—a suited designation of Old-Testament saints (Heb. xii. 23). There will be a new *earth*, in which dwelleth righteousness, as there is an "inheritance reserved in *heaven*" for believers now (1 Pet. i. 4; 2 Pet. iii. 13). I cannot dwell upon this here, and yet if it is not seen, there must be real and great confusion. But all in these different places are blood-washed ones alike: the same sacrifice has been made for all; His name under whom Judah shall be saved and Israel shall dwell safely will be, for them as for us, "The Lord our Righteousness" (Jer. xxiii. 6). Yet Israel's promises are earthly, and not heavenly. We see, then, that to have "Christ made unto us righteousness" involves no necessary place in heaven.

And yet the cross is the sufficient justification of whatever place can be given to a creature; and it has pleased God to take out of the Gentiles a people for His name, to make known the value of the cross and show forth the exceeding riches of His grace. In Christ we are already seated in the heavenly places, and where He is is to be our place forever. This we know; and it is part of the blessed plan in which God in Christ shall be fully made known, to the deepest joy and adoration of His creatures.

We are reminded here of the unequal offerings of the day of atonement,—the bullock for the priesthood, and the two goats for the nation of Israel. They are types of the same sacrifice, but in different aspects; and the priesthood clearly represent the heavenly family, as the holy place to which they belong represents the heavenly places themselves. We have considered this already, however, in its place.

And now we may close this brief and imperfect sketch of an all-important subject by reminding our readers of the way in which the Lamb—the atoning victim—fills the eye all through the book of Revelation. Not only by the blood of the Lamb the saints' robes are washed and the victors overcome; not only is it the Lamb that the redeemed celebrate, while the wicked dread His wrath; but He is the opener of the seven-sealed book, the interpreter of the divine counsels; His is the book of life, and the first-fruits from the earth, and the bride the Lamb's wife; the Lord God Almighty and the Lamb are the temple of the city; the glory of God lightens it, and the Lamb is the light; while the river of the water of life flows eternally from the throne of God and of the Lamb.

> "Soon shall our eyes behold Thee,
>   With rapture, face to face;
> One half hath not been told me
>   Of all Thy power and grace.
> Thy beauty, Lord, and glory,
>   The wonders of Thy love
> Shall be the endless story
>   Of all Thy saints above."

*F. W. G.*

www.ingramcontent.com/pod-product-compliance
Lightning Source LLC
Chambersburg PA
CBHW062026220426
43662CB00010B/1494